DYNAMITE
CHICKEN

FOOD52

DYNAMITE CHICKEN

60 NEVER-BORING RECIPES FOR YOUR FAVORITE BIRD

Tyler Kord

Photographs by
James Ransom

TEN SPEED PRESS
California | New York

Contents

WINNER, WINNER: WEEKNIGHT CHICKEN DINNERS

BIG, ARDUOUS, FULFILLING PROJECTS

PARTY CHICKEN TO IMPRESS GUESTS (& CELEBRITIES!)

CHICKEN TO EAT WHEN YOU ARE SAD

DISHES TO GET YOUR PICKY KIDS TO EAT REAL FOOD, CHICKEN EDITION

Foreword

One of the perks of starting a company is you get to do things your way. We close our office for two weeks a year. Because we can! We use table lamps on our desks instead of harsh overhead lighting. Because we like them! And we don't mindlessly feature boneless, skinless chicken breast recipes on our site. Because we don't think pandering to clicks will inspire and help people.

So if you'd asked us eight years ago if we'd ever do a chicken cookbook, we'd have said, "Never!" This wasn't reflexive snobbery. We like chicken! But it's become a default for many food publications, and we're determined to push ourselves (and you) in newer, more gratifying directions.

For years, our thoughtful and savvy publisher, Ten Speed Press, hinted that we should do a cookbook on chicken. Over time, our initial resistance gave way to amusement, then curiosity: *Could* we do a chicken cookbook we'd be proud of, one we'd want to buy ourselves? One with original ideas and exciting flavors, that was implicitly approachable without talking down to you? A cookbook that made chicken feel like an adventure?

We like a challenge. We also like surrounding ourselves with the best cooks and writers in the business. So we reached out to Tyler Kord, he of the amazingly titled cookbook *A Super Upsetting Cookbook About Sandwiches*. We were fans of Tyler's writing, and devotees of his No. 7 Sub shop, which he kindly located near our office. There, he makes delicious, rule-breaking sandwiches, like roasted broccoli with pickled lychee, and ham and cheese with pickled blueberries (and barbecue potato chips—on the sandwich).

We knew Tyler could write the anti-"chicken cookbook" chicken cookbook. And that he'd surprise us along the way by combining chicken with kimchi in pierogies. He'd make us laugh with a mash-up of chicken and lasagna—called Chickensagna, natch. And he'd raise the level of discourse around the appealing ease of chicken with a useful, intuitive Weeknight Chicken Dinner Matrix.

There are no chicken nuggets with ketchup here. But there *is* a chapter on time-consuming-yet-worth-it chicken recipes. And one on chicken for kids (they'll have their meatballs, but with giardiniera). So everyone can continue eating lots of chicken and never get bored—because there's no such thing as boredom when you're in Tyler's hands.

—Amanda Hesser & Merrill Stubbs, cofounders of Food52

Introduction

——

I am enamored of chicken. To me, it's the most delicious meat of all of the meats. Sure, steak's great, and who doesn't love bacon? (Except people who don't like bacon for extremely valid reasons separate from its deliciousness.) But chicken's affordability, versatility, and ease make it a clear favorite, and not just for me. Some of the world's most popular recipes involve chicken, from jerk chicken to chicken adobo to pho ga (Vietnamese chicken noodle soup). Heck, in my home state of New York, many of our favorite meals start with chicken. One dish, Buffalo wings, became one of the most famous foods on planet Earth! And there's Cornell Chicken, a barbecue dish beloved by my hometown—but we'll get to that in a minute.

So who am I? I'm a chef with a restaurant in Brooklyn called No. 7, and I'm often called "that broccoli guy" or "that sandwich guy" or "that broccoli sandwich guy." But we also proudly serve Cornell Chicken, fried chicken, and tons of chicken sandwiches. I'm also starting to admit I'm a writer: I wrote a book about sandwiches, one about broccoli, and sometimes I write articles that get nominated for James Beard Awards (okay, that happened once and I didn't win, and if you're bored, you can just skip to the recipes!).

What I'm not is someone who thinks there are "good" and "bad" ingredients. Chicken often gets drawn into this debate—are chicken legs or whole chickens better than boneless, skinless breasts? To me, the answer is no, so here you'll find recipes that excitedly embrace chicken in all its forms: whole-roasted birds, grilled wings, braised thighs, and—yes—boneless, skinless chicken breasts. In my view, this versatile cut is chicken's MVP, so we'll treat it with the finesse it deserves (like marinated in tahini-orange dressing, or nestled in buttery apple jam on toast).

Much as I love chicken, I recognize it can be a complicated ingredient. In the United States, these complications begin with Robert Baker, who taught at Cornell University's College of Agriculture and Life Sciences from 1957 to 1989. Baker was tasked with helping popularize chicken when a postwar nation needed to efficiently feed a whole lot more people. He invented chicken nuggets and poultry ham and bacon, as well as Cornell Chicken, and the country rejoiced! And while that's helped many families, who can now serve protein for a couple of dollars a pound, it's come with significant ethical dilemmas related to factory farming.

When I buy chicken, I prefer to get it directly from small farmers, so I'm supporting people who ethically and sustainably raise it. I avoid factory-farmed chicken because to me, factories aren't doing a good enough job of protecting our environment and ensuring there are no sketchy things in their meat. I usually shop at a butcher who sells chickens from small farms; since the meat costs more, I'm choosier about when I eat it, and try to use as much of the bird as I can. But this strategy may be tough and not realistic for everyone. At my local grocery, I've seen several options for meat raised without hormones or antibiotics, an alternative to consider. Though it's still factory-farmed, it can be more humane for the chickens (improved housing standards, in some cases) and better for us to eat (less sketchy stuff).

On the subject of responsibility, I want to point out something I think falls within my responsibility to you. While I perpetually look to ingredients and techniques from other places, I did my damnedest not to write easy, weeknight versions of complex chicken dishes from cultures that are not my own. I don't want to speak as a representative of a culture over which I don't have authority—I'd much rather leave that to the people who *do* have it, for whom a particular dish is an important signifier of their heritage. So you won't find Chicken Pad Thai or Chicken Tikka Masala here, but you will find Chicken & Kimchi Pierogies (page 71), and I think you'll really like them!

Complications aside, I still think you should eat chicken, the most delicious meat of all the meats. But while we're eating chicken, let's be thoughtful about it. I buy whole birds over individually wrapped pieces, to use less plastic and because I like all chicken parts. But if you aren't into that, buy prepackaged pieces; at the end of the day, I'd rather you do that than throw away parts you won't use. I get that it's a convenient way to buy chicken for individual meals, and there are plenty of recipes here where it makes sense to use cuts like this.

But if you can buy a whole chicken from a small farm, awesome—that one chicken can become three amazing meals. Use the breasts for spiced schnitzel on Tuesday (see page 16), poach the legs in a lemongrass broth on Thursday (see page 40), and make stock with the carcass on Friday (see page 9). Then use the stock for grits, to make tamales with those grits and leftover chicken on Saturday (see page 65). And I guess just eat broccoli all the other nights, like I do.

example, you cut chicken on a cutting board that you then use for something else without cleaning it first. I don't have a special chicken cutting board—I just wash my board and knife really well with hot, soapy water after cutting chicken on it. I also use standard antibacterial cleaning spray on the counter and sink after cutting chicken. I do not rinse chicken with water because that seems like an ineffective way to kill bacteria and a great way to simply splash bacteria all over the kitchen. Only cooking kills salmonella, and the government says to cook food to 165°F (75°C) to instantly pasteurize it. However, while cooking chicken breasts especially, I shoot for closer to 150°F (65°C) and try to hold it there for a couple minutes. This extra time at temp also leads to pasteurization, so your chicken breasts are safe to eat and won't dry out or get a little tough, like at 165°F (75°C)—but more on this below.

Super Important Fundamentals

This section will help you figure out the more technical aspects of cooking chicken, so that when you get to the recipes, you will already know everything I do! If you are a chicken expert, skip it, but know that you will also be skipping some pretty choice lines like, "Cooking chicken is like falling in love for the first time, every time." Actually, just read this section and learn so much about chicken!

CHICKEN SAFETY

I've cooked hundreds of chickens in my life, and I have never gotten salmonella poisoning. I suspect that the biggest culprit of salmonella is cross-contamination, which happens when, for

THE SUM OF ITS PARTS

Anybody who tells you that one part of the chicken is better than another part of the chicken is not somebody whose culinary advice you need to take too seriously. But even though it all comes from the same bird, chicken parts have different flavors and functions in recipes, and different cook times. Here's a guide to each of a chicken's parts, and how I like to cook them.

Chicken breasts are lean, texturally very consistent when cooked properly, and great for quick-cooking recipes. But they have less collagen and gelatin in them than the legs do, so if you cook them past 150°F (65°C) or so, they will release moisture and get dry and rubbery. Leave them on the bone if you want to give yourself a buffer on cook time, as this will help preserve moisture. Or cut them small and don't worry about perfection, as they can add great texture where a tender chicken leg can get lost. I like to sauté or gently poach chicken breasts.

Chicken legs, on the other hand, excel when cooked for a long time. The fat renders out and they get that juicy, shreddable, pulled-pork appeal. Use chicken legs when a recipe tells you to put the chicken in at the beginning and the dish has a total cooking time of 40 minutes. I find drumsticks and thighs to be pretty interchangeable, as they're both dark meat wrapped around a bone. The thigh is meatier, and the drumstick has a little more tendon action that you'll want to remove, but that is easy to do once the drumstick is cooked.

Chicken wings are delicious! They have a high skin-to-meat ratio, which lends itself to crispy roasted or fried preparations or nice charring on the grill. And they tend to be cheap and plentiful. That said, if you buy a whole chicken to cook for a few meals, it's probably not worth the effort of making just two Buffalo wings. Instead, you can put them in a pot with other chicken parts to make stock, and then they can become any number of things in spirit.

Now, if we're talking about boneless, skinless chicken, breast and thigh meat are relatively interchangeable. Pounded-out, quick-cooking recipes like chicken schnitzel (page 16) are great for breasts, whereas the long marinade and lengthier cook of chicken spiedies (page 134), while delicious with breasts, go even better with juicier thighs. I wouldn't necessarily say that the thighs have more flavor, but they have a slightly gamier profile worth keeping in mind.

BREAKING DOWN A CHICKEN

Cutting up a whole chicken into ten pieces is the best way to get relatively even portions of meat. When I say "ten pieces," I mean two wings, two drumsticks, two thighs, and four breast pieces. I use a sharp 8-inch chef's knife for everything— but it's not a crazy-expensive one, so I'm not worried about cutting through joints and bones with it. In the end, you'll have several pieces of bone-in chicken you can either cook together in a similar amount of time, or use somewhat interchangeably in various dishes.

You can store these parts in a clean airtight container in the coldest part of your fridge for 2 days. You can also divide them into quantities of your choosing (I'd go with servings of four, to match many of this book's recipes) and put those portions in individual ziplock freezer bags, manually pushing out all the air before sealing and freezing for up to 9 months. When you're ready to cook the precut chicken, first thaw it in the refrigerator for at least 5 hours per pound of meat, and up to 48 hours, before using.

Here's how I break down a chicken, starting with a whole bird (check out pages 4 and 5 for a handy visual).

Remove the Wings

First, check the chicken's cavity for any bag of neck bones and giblets that might be hanging out in there, removing it if there is one. Put the chicken on a cutting board, breast-side up, with its wingtips pointing to the right. Pull the wing closest to you toward you, and find where the wing meets the breast. Make a small slice at this point to reveal the joint, pop the joint out of its socket by applying pressure with your fingers, then slice toward the cutting board to cut cleanly through the joint, pulling the wing away from the breast. Rotate the chicken and repeat with the other wing.

Remove the Legs

The chicken's breasts should now be facing up and its legs should be pointing to your left. Pull the leg that's farther away from you slightly apart from the body, and slice into the natural partition of skin between the leg and the breast, until the inside of the leg is exposed. With your thumb on the inside of the leg, and your middle and ring fingers on the outside of the leg, where it meets the body, pull it away from the body, bending outward, until you feel the ball joint pop out of its socket. Flip the bird onto its side, so the breasts are facing you and the legs are pointing left. Hold the same leg you've been working with straight up into the air and pull the leg away from the body, letting the weight of the chicken's body fall. Begin to carve off the leg from right to left, by cutting first downward, toward the spine, and then across, parallel to it. Cut close to the chicken's back to make sure the oyster, a small and very tasty pocket of meat on either side of the spine, comes off with the leg. Pull the leg and oyster off. Rotate the chicken so the remaining leg is pointing right and repeat the process with the other leg.

Separate the Thigh and Drumstick

Put your knife on the chicken's leg, at the point where the drumstick and thigh meet. Make a small slice here to reveal the joint, and try again if you don't find the joint right away. When you find the joint, firmly slice straight through and separate the thigh from the drumstick. Repeat with the other leg.

Remove and Separate the Breasts

Orient the legless, wingless chicken so that the breasts are facing up and the bottom cavity is pointing to your right. Take your knife and put the blade up against the chicken's ribs, starting at the bottom cavity end, so it's parallel to the cutting board. Slice straight through horizontally, toward the opposite end of the chicken, until you reach its neck (the breast won't be fully cut off at this point). Lift up the breastplate like you're opening a book, exposing the joints where the chicken's neck, shoulders, and breastbone connect (this will be at the end you're not holding). Cut into each of the chicken's shoulder joints,

on either side of the breasts, down toward the cutting board, so you can completely remove the breastplate from the back.

Once removed, flip over the breasts so they're skin-side down on your cutting board. Push your knife firmly through the breastplate, straight down the middle, and separate the breasts from each other. Flip the breasts over, skin-side up, and halve them, cutting a little closer to the wide end than the narrow end so that each half has approximately the same amount of meat.

I WANT TO COOK CHICKEN RIGHT NOW, AND I DON'T WANT TO READ A WHOLE BOOK ABOUT IT

Several recipes in this book call for cooked chicken. While these are super excellent times to use up leftovers, if you don't have any or would rather cook fresh chicken, here are some very simple ways to achieve that.

Whole-Roasted Chicken

To roast a 3- to 4-pound (1.4 to 1.8kg) chicken, heat your oven to 400°F (200°C). Check the chicken's cavity for any bag of neck bones and giblets that might be hanging out in there, removing it if there is one. Then, season the chicken all over with plenty of kosher salt (so the salt can really make its way into the skin and meat), rub extra-virgin olive oil or vegetable oil on the skin (add more salt if it rubs off with the oil), put the chicken in a large roasting pan or on a sheet pan, and cook it in the oven for an hour. If the skin doesn't get dark enough while roasting, put the chicken under the broiler for a couple of minutes longer. If the chicken needs a little more than an hour to be done, give it an hour and 10 minutes and take note for next time.

BREAKING DOWN A CHICKEN

REMOVE THE WINGS.
Pull away from the body, pop the joint, and cut straight down.

REMOVE THE LEGS.
Gently slice through the skin between the leg and the breast. Grip the chicken's leg with your thumb on the inside, and bend the leg away from the body to pop the ball joint. Hold up the leg and carve it off, cutting close to the chicken's spine (and don't forget the oyster!).

REMOVE AND SEPARATE THE BREASTS.
Slice horizontally to separate the breastplate and back. Then cut straight down the middle, through the breastbone, and again across the widest part of the breast.

SEPARATE THE THIGH
AND DRUMSTICK.

Slice along the joint.

TA-DA!

Spatchcocking (or, The Art of Smooshing)

Spatchcocking a chicken is as easy as removing the spine and pressing the bird flat. It's a fun technique and gives you another option for cooking a whole bird—but let me be clear that this is not some magical secret to a perfect, evenly roasted chicken! What it *is* good for is saving time when you're roasting a chicken, or applying direct heat to a greater portion of the chicken's surface area. So this is the best move for grilling a whole chicken (see page 106) or roasting a chicken quickly and still achieving a crispy skin (see page 99).

To do the job, you can use sharp kitchen shears or a knife. If using shears, position the chicken so that the breasts are on the cutting board and the drumsticks are pointing accusingly at you as you stare into the empty cavity that once held all of the essential mechanisms of life. Insert the shears into the bottom cavity, on the left side of the backbone (step 1), and cut straight ahead of you along the bone, curving in a tiny bit to get around the oyster, and continuing on to the neck until you have cut all of the way through one side. Repeat on the right side of the backbone until you can completely remove it—the bone should be 1 to 1½ inches (3.5 to 3.8cm) in width (step 2). If you are using a knife, hold the chicken upright so its cavity is facing up and its back is facing you. Position your knife on the right side of the backbone and cut straight down, curving in a tiny bit to get around the oyster. Repeat on the left side of the backbone until you can completely remove it.

When you have removed the backbone, reserve it to make stock. Flip the chicken over, breast-side up, and spread it out, pressing down on the breastbone to flatten it (step 3). You may also cut the breastbone out from the inside and the chicken will sit even flatter. To do this, flip the flattened chicken over so that you are looking at the inside of the breastbone. With your knife, make slits along either side of the breastbone until you can pull it free.

STEP 3

STEP 2

STEP 1

Roasted Chicken Parts

Roasting bone-in, skin-on chicken parts is just like roasting a whole chicken! Heat the oven to 400°F (200°C), season the parts generously with kosher salt, rub with oil, and roast. The breasts should be done in 30 minutes and the legs in 45, so pull them out accordingly—the meat should be fully white in the middle, and not even a little pink. If the parts don't get brown on the outside, broil them for a few minutes to get extra-crispy and delightful skin.

Poached Chicken

Poaching chicken is quick and easy and leaves you with super tender meat and a little bit of flavorful stock to use for other things. Put four boneless chicken pieces (about 2 pounds, or 900g) in a pot and just barely cover them with water (about 1½ quarts, or 1.4L). Add 1½ teaspoons of kosher salt. Over medium-high heat, bring the water up to a light boil, turn the heat to low, and gently simmer the chicken in the broth until it is just cooked, 7 to 10 minutes. You can add onions, garlic, herbs—whatever you like—but those flavors will shine through more in the resulting broth than in the chicken itself.

Sautéed Chicken

Sautéing chicken is the fastest and arguably most delicious way to cook it, because you can get the most intense caramelization in a very short time. Simply heat a sauté pan on high heat with a little vegetable or extra-virgin olive oil until smoking, season chicken well with kosher salt, and place it in the pan, skin-side down (if working with skin-on chicken). Cook the chicken on that side without disturbing it until it is cooked almost all of the way through—5 to 7 minutes for a boneless breast, 18 to 20 minutes for a bone-in breast, and 28 to 30 minutes for thighs or drumsticks— lowering the heat to medium after 5 to 7 minutes for the bone-in pieces. It can be tricky to tell when

a bone-in chicken breast is almost cooked, so peek in between the breast and tenderloin and cook it until there's only a little pink left. Then flip and cook it for another minute or two until there is no more pink.

Broiled Chicken

Broiling chicken is fun and exciting—you get crispy skin and tender meat in an impossibly short time. That said, it's a pretty aggressive way to cook chicken, so I recommend you keep an eye on it because things happen pretty quickly. Season bone-in, skin-on chicken parts with kosher salt, rub the skin with vegetable or olive oil, put the pieces under the broiler, and flip them pretty regularly so that they don't burn— every 3 or 4 minutes. Depending on the size and thickness of your chicken, and the seriousness of your broiler, the parts should take between 8 and 12 minutes (or 25 to 30 for bigger pieces) to cook. To see if they're cooked, check the thickest part of the meat—if it's pink, it needs some more time, and if it's white throughout, it's fully cooked.

Shredded Chicken

Basically any of the preceding cooking preparations make good chicken for shredding, but poaching and broiling are the fastest and easiest ways to get there. First, cook the chicken in any of the ways mentioned. Then, to shred, transfer the cooked chicken to a plate or cutting board and let it cool until it can be handled easily, or ideally to room temperature, 10 to 20 minutes. Use your hands to pull the meat off of the bones and then shred it into small pieces; or using two forks, hold the chicken steady with one fork and scrape the chicken off the bone with the tines of the other to shred. Save or freeze any skin, bones, fat, or cartilage for stock (unless you like those things to be in your chicken salad), and you're ready to use the delicious shredded meat.

Let's Just Put the Chicken in the Oven

I used to think whole-roasting chickens was stupid because it meant making a choice between undercooked legs and perfectly cooked breasts, or perfectly cooked legs and overcooked breasts, so I would just roast the parts separately. But that just isn't as fun or as easy—and it turns out that the perfect way to cook a whole chicken is to stop caring so much about perfection. See below for my advice on whole-roasting chicken, including how to tell if your chicken is done. (Personally, I tend to err on the side of cooking the legs properly and getting the skin crispy, and accepting that the breast isn't going to be as juicy as if it were poached; instead, I have gravy and a positive mental attitude.)

When's My Chicken Done?

I find it troublesome to gauge a whole-roasted chicken's doneness using temperature because I have never figured out the correct place to stick a thermometer—when I put it in the breast, the thickest part of the chicken, either it will say 125°F (52°C) and the chicken is super overcooked, or it will say 175°F (80°C) and the chicken is still a little raw. And the juice thing? The juice coming out of a chicken is never clear, at 165°F (75°C) or otherwise. There is just too much biology going on in there. So I say wiggle the leg. Does it feel loose? Is the skin pulling back from the joint where the foot would have been attached? After an hour of cooking, is the skin super dark or is it still a little pale?

Once I'm ready to pull the chicken from the oven, I let it rest for 10 minutes and then slice into the thickest part—just to the side of the breastbone. If the meat is white and not pink, then we win! If it's not, it's rested only 10 minutes and the oven won't take long to heat back up, so back in it goes. I realize that cookbook authors and chefs, of which I am a strange combo, are supposed to give much more precise answers than that, but I am here to tell you guys the truth. And once you get to know how long it takes to cook a 4-pound (1.8kg) chicken at 400°F (200°C) in your oven, then you won't even need to think about thermometers or juices anymore!

Truss Issues

This might be an unpopular opinion, but to me, trussing is a sad attempt to combat the virtually inevitable discrepancy in cooking times between chicken legs and breasts. By pulling the legs and wings up to cover the bottom cavity, you're supposedly preventing hot air from circulating through the chicken. This abundance of hot air is what normally overcooks and dries out the breast before the legs are done. But even if it works, to me trussing misses the point of roasting a whole chicken in the first place—the ease. You have to do a bunch of work on the bird before you season it and put it in the oven, and it's not even easier to serve it when it's done. In fact, trussing makes things harder because you still have to untie it! People will tell you to truss a whole chicken for even roasting, but like I said before, if you want all of the different parts of a chicken to be cooked perfectly and be ready at exactly the same time, roasting the whole chicken is probably the last technique I would recommend.

ON CHICKEN STOCK

There are a lot of recipes in this book involving chicken stock because I love it. It is easy to make, it is full of amino acids for health, and, most important, it is super delicious. I always have some in my freezer, made with only three ingredients: chicken, water, and restraint. No roasting the bones, no carrots or celery or onions. Just pure chicken.

To make the very best chicken stock, simply put a whole 3- to 4-pound (1.4 to 1.8kg) chicken (and its neck, if you have it, but not the giblets) with all its bones into a large stockpot or pressure cooker, adding a few quarts of water (about a quart and a half for each pound of chicken). Cook this for an hour, skimming the surface occasionally in the stockpot, and straining the stock after cooking if using a pressure cooker. With a whole bird, you'll get a little gaminess from the dark meat, some distinct chickeniness from the white meat, and a little fattiness from the skin. The downside (or upside, depending) of making stock this way is that you will have a ton of meat on your hands afterward, and the white meat won't always stay tender. If you break down the chicken (see page 2) before making your stock, you can pull the white meat out as soon as it's cooked through, leaving the dark meat to keep cooking in the pot. But if that's too tricky, you can just learn to love chicken cooked in every different way, as I have!

Another way to make stock is with the bony parts: just bones themselves—maybe the ones left over from your roast chicken—or a combination of bones and super affordable raw wings, backs, necks, and feet. The resulting stock from either of these combinations will be full of richness and thickness from the gelatin in the bones.

So if you want to make a couple quarts of thick, rich stock and not end up with a pot of potentially overcooked chicken, try starting with a pound of bones and a pound of flavorful dark meat (like thighs or drumsticks).

If you happened to make a little bit too much stock or need only a small amount for your recipe, let it cool and freeze any leftovers in small containers. Filling ice cube trays with stock can be handy for when you need just a splash here and there. Two-cup portions are perfect if you've got the sniffles and need a quick batch of grocery store ramen (see page 128).

LEFTOVERS!!!

While a few recipes in this book call for cooked chicken, many more can give you great leftovers to use. The best leftovers come from bone-in chicken, cooked whole or in parts (like the Szechuan Pepper–Lacquered Chicken on page 74, or the Parmesan-Sake Grilled Chicken on page 48), because the bones allow the chicken to stay tender and moist without easily overcooking. Another great choice is poached boneless, skinless chicken because it stays pretty tender, too. And like I said earlier, if you make stock, you'll have a lot of chicken meat left on the bones; this meat won't have a ton of flavor by itself, but it's pretty great in recipes where you're adding another flavorful component—like with the dressing in the Meyer Lemon Chicken Salad Sandwiches (page 51), with Salsa Más Macha in some tamales (page 65), or with savory-sweet braised greens and chickeny oatmeal (page 116).

You can store leftover chicken in a sealed container in the fridge for about a week. Some people will say less and some people will say more. I say, just look at your leftovers and sniff them, and if they change color or smell weird, throw them away. And freezing cooked chicken is like freezing cooked anything—the more appropriately you portion it before freezing, the more useful it will be. I freeze leftovers in relatively small portions in ziplock freezer bags so that I can thaw out as much as I want. These frozen leftovers will last for several months.

NON-CHICKEN STAPLES TO MAKE CHICKEN TASTE (AND BE) BETTER

Every single chicken dish you make is like a glass of lemonade. That might sound dumb, but hear me out. Lemonade is pretty much always good, but if you strike the right balance of sweet, sour, bitter, and salty (yes, there should be just the tiniest bit of salt in lemonade), it can be the most delicious beverage in the (known) universe. The same is true of a plate of chicken. By tasting and tweaking acid, salt, and sugar, I tried to turn each of the dishes in this book into the most perfect glass of lemonade that I could. To do this, I often used two important ingredients: distilled white vinegar and maple syrup.

Vinegar—particularly, distilled white vinegar—is my favorite way to add brightening acid to a dish without adding additional and sometimes competing flavor. It basically goes incognito, which lets chicken do its thing, complementing its meatiness with a little bite. That said, any other mild-flavored vinegar (rice wine, white wine, champagne) or citrus juice (lemon and lime are my go-tos) could be good for your acidic element. To see vinegar in action, try the Chicken & Shrimp Dumplings (page 79) without a little pickled onion, and then some with it; I guarantee the taste between bites will be super different, and the one with the onion will highlight chicken's richness and gaminess even more.

Next, there's maple syrup, which most people reserve for pancakes. Even though maple syrup does have a distinct flavor, for whatever mystical reason it just blends into food in ways that I don't understand, and improves it by balancing and enhancing salty, sour, and bitter elements. Try making the Chicken & Broccoli Meatballs on page 154 without the maple syrup first, by mixing everything together, cooking off a tiny patty of the meat mixture in a sauté pan, and tasting it. Then mix in the syrup and cook it and try it again, and the difference will be crystal clear. Again, you'll taste the savory chickeniness even more when you add sweetness. Feel free to use sweeteners interchangeably—maple syrup, honey, brown sugar, molasses, or a sweetener I might not know about.

In addition to vinegar and maple syrup, one of my favorite ingredients to use in the kitchen is cornstarch. Cornstarch does two unique and important things for cooking: It makes fried things crispy for days, and it turns a loose sauce into thick velvet that will coat anything it touches. To maximize chicken crispiness, I rub it on the skin of the butterflied chicken on page 99 (a trick I learned from my old boss, Jean-Georges Vongerichten), and dredge pieces of chicken with it, like the fried-chicken croutons for the salad on page 102. Cornstarch also makes a righteous gravy see pages 48 and 98, so I use it that way, too, with homemade chicken stock.

Rotisserie Chicken Beans (aka The Only Thing That Tyler Kord Would Eat If Left to His Own Devices)

Serves 4

One 3-pound rotisserie chicken (1.4kg), or roast chicken from page 35

6 cups (1.4L) water, plus more as needed

½ onion

1 carrot

½ bunch cilantro (stems and leaves)

1 cup (175g) dried beans of your choosing, not soaked

1 teaspoon kosher salt

½ tablespoon unsalted butter

Bread or cooked rice, lime wedges, and hot sauce, for serving

Look, I know this isn't a chicken fundamental, in that it uses a rotisserie chicken and we don't even make that in this book. But chicken and beans are so entwined in my mind that I couldn't let the book be published without this recipe. It's an awesome way to hydrate a bag of what are essentially rocks with super-concentrated chicken flavor, and to me, it's what cooking with chicken is all about: transforming seemingly boring ingredients, like dried beans, into a finished pot of food that transcends what you started with. But also I just really like beans.

1. Pull all the meat off the chicken and put all of your meat and scraps, including the skin and bones, into a pot or pressure cooker. Pour the water over the bones, bring to a boil over high heat, turn the heat to low, and simmer for 1 to 2 hours, making sure to add water occasionally to maintain the starting level of 6 cups (1.4L).

2. While the stock is cooking, peel and chop the onion and carrot into ½-inch (1.3cm) pieces, chop the cilantro, and watch the first half of *Casablanca*. You're done chopping and the problems of three little chickens don't amount to a pot of beans in this crazy world. Someday you'll understand that.

3. When the stock is awesome (and feel free to refer back to the discussion of stock on page 9), strain it and reserve the shredded chicken. Return the strained stock to the same pot (you should have about 6 cups/1.4L), and add the beans and salt. Bring the beans up to a boil, turn the heat to low, and cover.

4. As the beans cook and absorb the stock, add a little bit of water to maintain the level of liquid that you started with. Once the beans are almost cooked (between 1 and 2 hours), add the onion and carrot and either start to reduce the broth to ever so slightly thicken the sauce, or mash some of the beans to more substantially thicken it. I like both options, but if you go with the first, don't reduce too much so you keep the beans super saucy. Once your beans are properly creamy and amazing (even if some of them have fallen apart), take the pot off the heat and add the reserved shredded chicken, cilantro, and butter. Serve the stew with some bread or rice to soak up the broth, a lime wedge to squeeze over it all, and some hot sauce, because hot sauce is usually the best idea.

Winner, Winner: Weeknight Chicken Dinners

Broiled Chicken Thighs with Plum Tomatoes & Garlic

Serves 4

2 pounds (900g) bone-in, skin-on chicken thighs

2 teaspoons extra-virgin olive oil

2 teaspoons kosher salt

6 plum tomatoes, halved

10 garlic cloves, smashed

12 sprigs (7g) fresh thyme

1 tablespoon white wine vinegar

1 teaspoon fish sauce

Bread, for serving

This recipe is loosely based on Merrill Stubbs's Braised Chicken Thighs with Tomato and Garlic, and it's one of the most delicious things I have ever cooked. That's not hyperbole! The charred thyme makes the chicken taste like it came out of a wood-burning oven at a fancy restaurant, and the fish sauce, while subtle, adds a powerful dimension of flavor. The dish is so quick, easy, and satisfying that it will now make a regular appearance on my table. I prefer to cook the thighs with the bones in, but like to remove them just before serving. To do this, I recommend cutting along the bones while the chicken is raw to make them easier to take out after the thighs are cooked—just run a sharp paring knife along either side of each bone without slicing all the way through.

1. Heat the oven to 400°F (200°C). In a roasting pan, toss the chicken thighs with the oil and 1½ teaspoons of the salt. Roast for 45 minutes, or until the thighs are nicely browned but not too dark.

2. Remove the roasting pan from the oven and turn on the broiler setting to high. Add the tomatoes and garlic and toss with the roasted chicken. Redistribute the chicken, tomatoes, and garlic evenly in the pan and arrange the thyme sprigs over the top. Position the pan directly under the broiler and broil for 4 to 8 minutes, or until the thyme is very charred, the chicken skin is a little charred, and the tomatoes and garlic are starting to brown at the edges.

3. Remove the pan from the oven and separate out the chicken thighs, resting them on a plate. Put the tomatoes and garlic in a bowl (and spoon in any pan drippings), pulling out any thyme stems that survived the broiler (most of them should have burnt and kind of disintegrated into the tomatoes). Add the vinegar, fish sauce, and remaining ½ teaspoon salt and toss everything together. The mixture will be saucy.

4. Put the chicken thighs on a platter (deboned and sliced, if you feel like it) and surround with the tomatoes, garlic, and juices, and serve with crusty bread on the side.

Spiced Chicken Schnitzel

Serves 4

4 boneless, skinless chicken breasts, about 2 pounds (900g)

2 cups (250g) all-purpose flour

2 teaspoons kosher salt

2 eggs, beaten

½ cup (120ml) water

¼ cup (60ml) white wine vinegar

3 cups (150g) panko bread crumbs

½ cup (120ml) vegetable oil

2 teaspoons cumin seeds

2 teaspoons coriander seeds

½ teaspoon red pepper flakes

Salad

2 tablespoons minced shallots

2 tablespoons extra-virgin olive oil

2 teaspoons white wine vinegar

1 teaspoon kosher salt

4 cups (80g) baby arugula

1 fennel bulb, thinly sliced

1 apple, such as McIntosh or Fuji, cored and thinly sliced

1 lemon, cut into 8 wedges, for squeezing

I am not one of those people who think that carbohydrates are bad. I would gladly eat mashed potato sandwiches over rice, smothered in gravy. So in the rare cases my wife and I have salad for dinner, it's usually on top of a large piece of carb-covered chicken schnitzel, because we can. Here, pounded, breaded, pan-fried chicken breast is spiced with cumin and coriander *after* it's cooked, to add toasty nuttiness from the chicken's residual heat without accidentally burning the spices. Try squeezing a lemon over the whole dish, and suddenly you'll want to squeeze lemons over everything in your life.

1. It's time to pound the chicken! Place one breast into a big piece of plastic wrap and fold over, leaving plenty of room around the edges. Using the smooth side of a meat hammer or the flat bottom of a pan, repeatedly hit the chicken, working in a circular motion around it. The breast should be double in size (and approximately ½ inch/1.3cm thick). Repeat with the remaining breasts.

2. On a large plate with a lip, mix the flour and 1 teaspoon of the salt. In a wide shallow bowl, whisk together the eggs, water, and vinegar. Place the panko in another plate with a lip. Take a chicken breast and dredge it in the flour mixture, coating it completely. Next, place it in the egg liquid, and finally lay it in the panko, coating both sides. Repeat with the remaining breasts.

3. Heat ¼ cup (60ml) of the oil in your largest sauté pan over medium-high heat until almost smoking, and gently put two pieces of breaded chicken in the pan. Fry until golden brown, turning once, 4 minutes per side; lower the heat if they're browning too quickly. Transfer to a paper towel–lined plate to drain, and heat the remaining ¼ cup (60ml) oil in the pan until almost smoking. Fry/drain the remaining chicken as above. While the second batch is cooking, mix the remaining 1 teaspoon salt with the cumin, coriander, and red pepper flakes in a small bowl (crushing the seeds with a mortar and pestle, if you prefer) and season the finished breasts with half of the mixture, using the rest for the second batch once cooked.

4. Right before serving, make the salad: In a large bowl, whisk together the shallots, oil, vinegar, and salt. Add the arugula, fennel, and apple and toss with the dressing.

5. Put each chicken breast on a plate and divide the salad evenly, piling it on the chicken. Serve with the lemon wedges and make sure that everybody squeezes some on or they have to go straight to bed.

Farfalle with Chicken, Broccoli & All of the Herbs

Serves 4

1 head broccoli, chopped into medium florets, stems thinly sliced

8 garlic cloves, lightly smashed

2 boneless, skinless chicken breasts, about 1 pound (450g)

2 tablespoons extra-virgin olive oil

3 teaspoons kosher salt

8 ounces (225g) farfalle

3 cups (710ml) chicken stock

½ cinnamon stick

1 star anise

½ tablespoon unsalted butter

2 ounces (55g) Parmesan, grated

¼ cup (10g) fresh dill fronds, coarsely chopped

¼ cup (10g) fresh basil leaves, coarsely chopped

¼ cup (10g) fresh tarragon leaves, coarsely chopped

¼ cup (10g) fresh mint leaves, coarsely chopped

A few of my Italian friends think that chicken in pasta is gross and stupid, and that is totally inexplicable to me. Meaty ragus are commonplace in Italy, so I'm not sure why chicken in pasta is taboo. My vote is that we just go ahead and put chicken in our pasta and not worry about what anybody thinks of it. This pasta (with chicken) is unlike any weeknight pasta you've ever had. It's a nod toward cacio e pepe, but instead of making a sauce from the pasta cooking liquid and black pepper, we are using garlicky chicken stock with a subtle hint of cinnamon and star anise. There is also the roast chicken and charred broccoli and fresh herbs to make it feel like we're not just eating pasta for the millionth night in a row—not that there's anything wrong with that!

1. Heat the oven to 450°F (230°C).

2. In a roasting pan, combine the broccoli, garlic, chicken breasts, oil, and 2 teaspoons of the salt. Toss everything well and spread out evenly in the pan. Roast for about 20 minutes, or until the broccoli is a little charred on the edges, the garlic is a little brown, and the chicken is no longer pink. Pull the pan out of the oven and put the chicken on a plate to cool. Put the roasted garlic in a large sauté pan.

3. In a large pot, boil enough water to cook the pasta. Add the pasta to the boiling water and cook for about two-thirds of the time recommended on the package (5 to 6 minutes).

4. While the pasta is cooking, add the stock, cinnamon, star anise, and remaining 1 teaspoon salt to the pan with the garlic, bring it to a boil, and lower the heat to a simmer. Shred the cooked chicken.

5. Drain the par-cooked pasta (reserving some of the cooking water) and add it to the pan with the stock. Increase the heat to high and cook the pasta for another 5 to 6 minutes, stirring regularly. When the pasta is a minute away from being done, add the broccoli and chicken and stir well to combine. The pasta will have absorbed some of the liquid and the stock will have reduced, but there should still be a cup or so of liquid in the pan; if not, add some pasta cooking water or chicken stock.

6. Turn off the heat and add the butter, Parmesan, and herbs, stirring well until the butter and cheese are melted. Remove and discard the cinnamon and star anise before serving.

Grilled Chicken with Pickled Blueberry Salad

Serves 4

Pickled Blueberries

½ cup (120ml) distilled white vinegar

1 teaspoon granulated sugar

1 teaspoon kosher salt

¼ cup (60ml) water

1 cup (150g) blueberries

¼ small red onion, thinly sliced

Harissa Kewpie Mayo

3 tablespoons Kewpie mayonnaise

½ teaspoon harissa paste

Vinaigrette

2 tablespoons blueberry pickle brine

1 tablespoon extra-virgin olive oil

¼ teaspoon kosher salt

1 cup (20g) arugula

½ cup (75g) crumbled feta

Chicken

4 boneless, skinless chicken breasts, about 2 pounds (900g)

1 tablespoon extra-virgin olive oil

1 teaspoon kosher salt

1 teaspoon fresh thyme leaves

In this dish, we'll pound chicken breasts, marinate them with fresh thyme, and grill them. I'm pretty sure that when thyme chars, special antioxidants are released into the air that kill any bad vibes and make your grilled chicken even better. Then, we have harissa, a Tunisian roasted chile paste, folded into sweet-and-savory Kewpie mayo to make one of the most righteous sauces known to humankind. And last, we have pickled blueberries. I think of blueberries as smaller, sweeter, bluer versions of the sweetest cherry tomatoes of the summer, and often use them interchangeably. Mixed with arugula and feta cheese, they are the brightest way to top a plate of delicious grilled chicken!

1. To make the pickled blueberries, combine the vinegar, sugar, salt, and water in a mixing bowl and whisk until the sugar and salt are completely dissolved. Add the blueberries and red onion, stir well to combine, and transfer the mixture with its brine to a nonreactive container with a lid. Refrigerate for at least 1 hour and up to 2 weeks.

2. Heat the grill to the temperature of planet Earth's molten core, or just to high. Meanwhile, to make the harissa Kewpie mayo, combine the mayo and harissa in a small bowl, mix well until combined, and set aside.

3. Onto the vinaigrette. In a small mixing bowl, whisk together the blueberry brine, oil, and salt. In a separate bowl, combine the arugula, feta, and ½ cup of the pickled blueberries and onions, drained. The chicken will cook quickly, so you want everything ready to go so you can toss it together when the chicken is done.

4. To pound out the chicken, place one breast into a big piece of plastic wrap and fold over, leaving plenty of room around the edges. Using the smooth side of a meat hammer or the flat bottom of a pan, repeatedly hit the chicken, working in a circular motion around it. The finished chicken should be double in size (and approximately ½ inch/1.3cm thick). Repeat with the remaining breasts. Season the chicken evenly with the oil, salt, and thyme. Put it in a single layer on the grill, searing on one side until almost completely cooked through, 7 to 10 minutes. Flip and cook for another 2 to 3 minutes, just until no longer pink, and transfer to a plate.

5. Spread about a tablespoon of the mayo on each chicken breast. Toss the salad with the vinaigrette, top each breast with a handful, and serve.

Spicy Chocolate Milk–Simmered Chicken

Serves 4

1 cup (240ml) full-fat chocolate milk

2 tablespoons chili powder (I prefer the one made from ancho chiles)

2 jalapeños, stemmed and split lengthwise

2½ teaspoons kosher salt

4 bone-in, skin-on chicken thighs, about 1½ pounds (680g)

2 teaspoons extra-virgin olive oil

2 zucchini, sliced into ½-inch-thick (1.3cm-thick) rounds

2 garlic cloves, minced

Cooked quinoa, for serving

I know what you're thinking: "Oh wow, chocolate milk and chicken are finally coming together and now my life is complete." For all two of you not thinking that right now, let me tell you why the combo works.

1. Chicken poached in milk is absolutely wonderful, as evidenced by chicken potpie or any creamy chicken dish for that matter.
2. Chicken in a sweet sauce is totally a thing. See American Chinese food classics like sweet-and-sour chicken, General Tso's chicken, and orange chicken.
3. Chicken and chile and chocolate have a long and beautiful history in the form of mole, from the state of Puebla, Mexico.

So accept that this chicken may just be one of the most interesting and weird-good things you will make from a cookbook. After poaching the chicken (and I promise the milk will not curdle—the chocolate and Saturn's influence, even if you have only a low-level association with the ice giant's great powers, help keep it emulsified and beautiful), pull the meat out of the liquid and put it over quinoa with some sautéed zucchini for a solid weeknight meal. Or stuff it in corn tortillas with a spoonful of the braising liquid and Greek yogurt. Or, if you're feeling super amazing, pull the cooked chicken off the bones, add it to some cooked potatoes in a savory pie crust with some or all of the braising liquid, and bake the damn thing!

1. In a saucepan, combine the chocolate milk, chili powder, jalapeños, 2 teaspoons of the salt, and the chicken thighs. Bring the mixture to a boil over high heat, turn the heat to low, and simmer for 35 to 40 minutes, or until the chicken is very tender.

2. While the chicken is cooking, add the oil to a large sauté pan over high heat. When the oil just starts to smoke, add the zucchini and the remaining ½ teaspoon salt, and sauté for 5 to 7 minutes, stirring occasionally, until the zucchini is caramelized and soft, though not so soft that it's turning to mush. Add the garlic and cook for another minute, until the garlic starts to caramelize a little.

3. Serve the chicken and zucchini over cooked quinoa.

Roasted Drumsticks with Brussels Sprouts, Fennel & Jalapeño

Serves 4

8 chicken drumsticks, about 2 pounds (900g)

8 ounces (225g) brussels sprouts, halved

1 fennel bulb, thinly sliced

1 tablespoon kosher salt, plus ½ teaspoon

5 tablespoons vegetable oil

2 jalapeños, stemmed and cut into a few pieces

1 cup (150g) crumbled feta

⅓ cup (45g) pitted green olives, such as Castelvetrano, sliced into thin rounds

¼ cup fried shallots (store-bought work great)

I realize putting things on a sheet pan to make the oven equivalent of a one-pot meal is very on-trend right now and may go out of fashion someday. But the roasted chicken drumsticks and vegetables covered in gnarly feta cheese; briny olives; crunchy, savory fried shallots; and spicy jalapeño oil that go on this sheet pan should always be on-trend, because delicious things are forever. (Except, of course, aspic, or clarified and chilled meat Jell-O, which is super tasty but may never be trendy again. In the sequel to this book, *Chicken Stock and the Order of the Carcass*—self-published, 2034—we will dive deep into all of the delicious and untrendy things one can achieve with cold meat and gelatin.) Really, you could cover a rain boot in gnarly feta cheese; briny olives; crunchy, savory fried shallots; and spicy jalapeño oil and it would be outrageously delicious.

1. Heat the oven to 400°F (200°C).

2. In a large mixing bowl, toss together the drumsticks, brussels sprouts, fennel, 1 tablespoon salt, and 2 tablespoons of the oil until the chicken is all evenly coated. Spread everything out on a half sheet pan (or divide it up onto two sheet pans for maximum crispiness), making sure the chicken is not hiding under any of the vegetables. Roast for 30 to 35 minutes, or until the chicken is no longer pink and everything is caramelized and beautiful.

3. While the chicken and vegetables are roasting, put the jalapeños, remaining 3 tablespoons oil, and remaining ½ teaspoon salt in a blender and puree on high for so long that people come from other rooms of the house to see what you are doing (3 to 5 minutes). The contents of the blender should have heated up during this time, and if you crack the lid open you may see steam come out. We've essentially cooked the jalapeños with the residual heat from the blender's motor, which mellows out their spice and preserves their bright green color. Transfer the oil to a small metal bowl and refrigerate to cool it down quickly.

4. Remove the sheet pan from the oven, drizzle with the jalapeño oil, and top with the feta, olives, and fried shallots. Divide the drumsticks between four plates, with a big scoop of the vegetables on each. You'll need a knife and fork for this one.

Pan-Seared Chicken Thighs
with Newfangled Sauce

Serves 4

4 bone-in, skin-on chicken thighs, about 1½ pounds (680g)

2½ teaspoons kosher salt

1 teaspoon extra-virgin olive oil

8 ounces (225g) kabocha or butternut squash, peeled, seeded, and cut into ¼-inch (6.3mm) cubes

1 tablespoon Sambuca, dry vermouth, or sweet white wine

¾ cup (175ml) water or chicken stock

2 heads baby bok choy, cut into ½-inch (1.3cm) pieces

4 ounces (115g) goat cheese

Pan-searing chicken thighs gives them a whole lot of flavor in a short amount of time. We'll first get the skin crispy but finish cooking the chicken with tender vegetables, to give it extra time to render as much fat as possible—getting it somewhere between sautéed and braised. Sweet kabocha squash and bok choy come together as a surprising (but amazing) base for the juicy chicken thighs. To make the sauce that goes with it all, we'll use Sambuca—an anise-flavored liqueur that's often served with coffee at Italian restaurants, which brings an awesome flavor that amplifies the natural sweetness of the kabocha squash—and melt some funky goat cheese for creaminess. And oh, what a sauce!!! It's so good that I just googled "Goat Cheese and Sambuca Sauce," and it does not appear to be a thing, but maybe it can be now?

1. In a small mixing bowl, toss the chicken with ½ teaspoon of the salt. Heat the oil in a large sauté pan over high heat until smoking. Add the chicken thighs, skin-side down, and sauté for 10 minutes, lowering the heat a little if they are getting too dark, until the skin is crispy, brown, and spectacular. Flip the chicken thighs, push them out to the edges of the pan, turn the heat to medium, and continue cooking.

2. In the same mixing bowl you used for the chicken, toss the squash with 1 teaspoon of the salt and add to the pan with the chicken. Spread the squash out in the middle of the pan and cook, stirring occasionally, for 15 minutes, or until tender and nicely caramelized. Set aside the cooked chicken and squash on a plate.

3. Add the Sambuca to the pan and deglaze, scraping up the browned bits with a wooden spoon. Once the Sambuca is fully evaporated, add the water. Bring the water to a boil and add the bok choy, goat cheese, and the remaining 1 teaspoon salt. Stir until everything is combined and cook for another minute, until the goat cheese is fully melted into the sauce and the bok choy is a tiny bit wilted—bright green and still pretty crunchy.

4. Add the chicken and squash back to the pan. Cook for 1 minute, then check out the skin of your chicken thighs. If the skin doesn't feel crisped up enough for you, feel free to put it under the broiler for a couple of minutes (but know that this uncrispiness is a texture that I love, and we all need to embrace it more).

Warm Chicken & Potato Salad with Bacon Vinaigrette

Serves 4

4 red potatoes, cut into 1-inch (2.5cm) chunks

1 tablespoon kosher salt, plus 1 teaspoon

4 ounces (115g) bacon, cut crosswise into ½-inch (1.3cm) strips

1 teaspoon vegetable oil (optional)

1 pound (450g) boneless, skinless chicken breasts or thighs, cut into 1-inch (2.5cm) chunks

2 scallions, white and green parts, sliced thinly

¼ cup (60ml) black vinegar

2 tablespoons tahini

1 teaspoon chopped garlic

1 head Bibb or Boston lettuce, cored

There is a reason that some people eat nothing but meat and potatoes (possibly because that is what our bodies are primarily composed of), and this meat-and-potato salad allows you to satisfy that urge without seeming like the kind of person who eats nothing but meat and potatoes. It has chunks of tender chicken; creamy potatoes; a healthy amount of savory scallions and bacon; and some sweet and crunchy Bibb lettuce. And the vinaigrette is amazing! The idea for it comes from my friend Elena, who once texted me just to say that she had dressed a salad with a combination of tahini and the hot sauce we make in our restaurant, and it blew my mind a little. Mainly because most of my incoming texts are letting me know that a refrigerator is broken or that we received a letter from a lawyer's office that I should probably open. But also because it turns out that the earthy bitterness of the tahini balanced beautifully with the sweetness and acidity of the hot sauce— a gastrique of caramel and Chinese black vinegar with a ton of garlic and chiles that I won't make you buy for the purposes of this recipe. Instead, we'll use it as inspiration for a simpler, less spicy, but equally tart, sweet, and complex dressing that goes great with meat and potatoes.

1. Put the potatoes in a small pot and add enough water to cover them. Add the 1 tablespoon salt to the water, bring to a boil over high heat, turn the heat to medium, and simmer the potatoes until very tender but not falling apart, 7 to 10 minutes. Drain the potatoes and let them sit and dry out a little while you prep the rest of the salad.

2. While the potatoes are boiling, put the bacon in a large sauté pan over medium heat, adding the oil if needed. (If your bacon is more than about 50 percent fat, you don't really need the oil unless you want this to be super rich.) Cook the bacon until well rendered, crispy, and slightly brown, 5 to 7 minutes. Remove the bacon from the pan with a slotted spoon and set aside. Add the chicken and the remaining 1 teaspoon salt to the pan with the bacon fat and cook, stirring occasionally, until the chicken is no longer pink, 7 to 10 minutes. Turn off the heat and add the potatoes to the pan.

3. In a small mixing bowl, combine the reserved bacon, scallions, vinegar, tahini, and garlic and whisk well. Place some lettuce leaves on each plate, top with some potatoes and chicken, and drizzle over some of the vinaigrette to serve.

Crispy Chicken Thighs with Brown Butter & Radicchio

Serves 2

2 bone-in, skin-on chicken thighs, about ¾ pound (340g)

½ teaspoon kosher salt

½ teaspoon extra-virgin olive oil, plus more as needed

1 small head radicchio, cut in half through the core, and then each half cut into 3 even wedges, still connected by the core; or 3 red Belgian endives, split lengthwise

2 tablespoons unsalted butter

2 tablespoons freshly squeezed lemon juice

2 tablespoons water

2 tablespoons golden raisins

1 tablespoon drained capers

This dish is super simple to prep and comes together quickly, so it's perfect for a weeknight meal that's just a little fancy. Slightly bitter, totally delicious radicchio, the grapefruit of the vegetable world, is sautéed in wedges with chicken thighs. It's all finished with a sauce of chicken pan drippings, brown butter, lemon juice, capers, and golden raisins, which might be the greatest way on Earth to cook all of the above. Starting the chicken in a cold pan allows the fat to render slowly, getting the skin extra crispy as it cooks in more and more of its own rendered fat. You can easily double this recipe, but the chicken thighs and radicchio require a lot of surface area to get the crispiest, and I don't have a pan that big. But if you do, you'll have double the magic of chicken thighs that taste a little like radicchio and radicchio that tastes a little like chicken and a ton of food that all tastes like lemony brown butter.

1. Season the chicken thighs with ¼ teaspoon of the salt. In a large, cold sauté pan, add the oil and the thighs, skin-side down, so the skin is totally covered with the oil. Turn the heat to medium-high and cook until the thighs start to sizzle, 3 to 5 minutes. Turn the heat to low, move the thighs around to prevent sticking, and sauté until they have cooked most of the way through, about 25 minutes; the meat will turn white up the sides and toward the center on top.

2. Move the chicken to the side of the pan and sprinkle the remaining ¼ teaspoon salt onto that empty space, making sure there is plenty of chicken fat underneath it (add a little more oil if needed). Place the radicchio, cut-side down, in the pan on top of the salt. Increase the heat to medium and cook until the radicchio has browned and the chicken skin looks dark and crispy, 5 to 7 minutes.

3. Flip the chicken, leaving the radicchio for now, and add the butter to the pan. Let the butter brown for about 2 minutes (it will foam first, then subside and smell super nutty). Add the lemon juice, water, raisins, and capers and slightly swirl the pan to mix. Flip the radicchio and cook until the sauce thickens enough to coat the back of a spoon, 3 to 5 minutes. If it looks like it is cooking too quickly and the sauce might break, lower the heat. We want the raisins to hydrate and the sauce to nicely emulsify, which won't take long.

4. Put a few wedges of radicchio on each plate, top with a chicken thigh, spoon over the pan sauce, and serve.

Chopped Chicken Salad with Watermelon & Ricotta Salata

Serves 4 as an appetizer or 2 as an entrée

Croutons

2 thick slices bread (preferably crusty), cut into ½-inch (1.3cm) chunks (about 1 cup, or 60g)

1 garlic clove, minced

1½ teaspoons extra-virgin olive oil

¼ teaspoon dried oregano

Pinch of kosher salt

Vinaigrette

½ small shallot, minced

2 tablespoons white wine vinegar

1 tablespoon extra-virgin olive oil

1½ teaspoons kosher salt

1 teaspoon Dijon mustard

½ teaspoon honey

5 to 6 ounces (140 to 170g) cooked chicken, cut into ½-inch (1.3cm) chunks (about 1 cup)

4½ (130g) ounces watermelon, seeds removed, cut into ½-inch (1.3cm) chunks

2¼ (60g) ricotta salata or feta, cut into ½-inch (1.3cm) chunks

1 head escarole, cut into ½-inch (1.3cm) ribbons

I'm not usually a huge salad person, but when there are chicken and croutons and cheese involved, I am a super-huge salad person. And, as luck would have it, this salad involves chicken, croutons, and cheese! It is all kinds of crunchy, with sweetness from watermelon, but is balanced by funky, salty ricotta salata and a bright, shalloty vinaigrette. Any kind of leftover chicken is great here—I recommend roast chicken (page 35) or fried chicken (page 61)—or you can start from scratch with broiled or poached chicken (page 7). Make this in the summer when watermelons are at their juiciest, or conversely, make this in the winter when all you can think about is juicy summer watermelon but can find only bland, underripened, watery winter watermelon. (Just kidding!) Try any juicy and delicious fruit that's in season when you can't find watermelon, like blood oranges or persimmons. Just toss it with some chicken, cheese, croutons, and greens, and everything will be okay!

1. To make the croutons, heat the oven to 400°F (200°C). In a bowl, toss together the bread, garlic, oil, oregano, and salt until the bread is evenly coated. Spread out the croutons on a rimmed sheet pan and bake, tossing occasionally, until the croutons are browned and crunchy, about 10 minutes. Let cool while you make the vinaigrette and salad.

2. To make the vinaigrette, combine the shallot, vinegar, oil, salt, mustard, and honey in a small jar with a lid and give it a good shake to mix together.

3. Combine the chicken, watermelon, ricotta salata, escarole, croutons, and all of the vinaigrette in a bowl and toss well. Transfer to a serving platter or divide between plates and serve.

Roast Chicken with All of the Vegetables in Your CSA

Serves 4, even though it looks like way too many vegetables

One 3- to 4-pound (1.4 to 1.8kg) chicken

5 teaspoons extra-virgin olive oil, plus more for drizzling

3½ teaspoons kosher salt

4 large russet potatoes

2 small red cabbages

2 cups (280g) English peas (fresh, or frozen and thawed)

I know, I know—a recipe for roasting chicken that takes over an hour is billed as a Simple Weeknight Meal. But it's just so hands-off and satisfying that I would call this a Simple *Thursday* Night Meal. Meaning that it's easy but also gives you enough time to sip an extra martini, because it feels like your week may never end. And the hour-plus is all in the oven. As soon as the oven is hot (and frankly, there is no rule that says you can't put food in your oven before it is completely heated), you can stick in the chicken, and the vegetables can be prepped while it's cooking and thrown in as they are needed. If it looks like there are way too many vegetables, there are not. Your spouse or roommate or pet or parent may be saying, "That's too much, we're never going to eat all of that," but make them a second martini and tell them everything will be okay. Trust me.

1. Heat the oven to 400°F (200°C) and position the oven rack 4 to 6 inches from the broiler. To quarter the chicken, first cut out the spine as if you were spatchcocking it (see page 6). Then, make shallow slits on either side of the breastbone to loosen it, but instead of removing the breastbone, like we do when we spatchcock, simply cut directly through it, splitting the chicken in half lengthwise. Then, cut through the skin separating the thighs from the breast to make quarters.

2. In a large bowl, toss the chicken with 1 teaspoon of the oil and 1 teaspoon of the salt. Place the chicken, skin-side up, in a large roasting pan and put it in the oven. Now set a timer on your phone for 5 minutes!

3. Cut the potatoes, unpeeled, into 1-inch (2.5cm) cubes. In the same large bowl as the chicken, toss them with 2 teaspoons of the oil and 1 teaspoon of the salt. When the timer goes off, toss the potatoes into the pan with the chicken, and if you want to be truly awesome, place them peel-side down so they won't stick to the pan. Set another timer for 25 minutes.

4. Core the cabbages and cut them into 1-inch (2.5cm) chunks. Toss them with the remaining 2 teaspoons oil and 1 teaspoon of the salt in our favorite large bowl and add to the roasting pan when the timer goes off again. Use a

CONTINUED

spatula to free the chicken from the pan if it is sticking and give everything
a good toss. Set a final timer for 30 minutes more.

5. Throw the peas into the bowl with the remaining ½ teaspoon salt, letting
them just pick up what is left in there. When the timer goes off for the last time,
add them to the roasting pan and turn the broiler to high. Broil the chicken and
vegetables until everything is dark around the edges, 3 to 5 minutes, depending
on how intense your broiler is and how close the pan is to it.

6. Scoop the vegetables onto four plates and top with a triumphant chicken
piece. Finish with a light sprinkle of salt and a tiny drizzle of oil.

Tip:
———————

You could really use just about any vegetable under the sun for this dish, but you
will want to consider how long it takes to roast to perfection—use the chart on
the opposite page to guide you.

The Miraculous Chart of Chicken & Vegetable Roasting, Based on How Tyler Prefers Them to Be Cooked

Once you start your chicken, you can throw all of your vegetables into the oven at the same time if you'd like, but they come out better if you do it in stages; if not, the cabbage will burn by the time the potatoes are cooked, and the peas will be pretty upsetting. So here is a handy chart for when to put different vegetables into the oven (where it makes sense, cut them into 1-inch/2.5-cm chunks). It's based on a 65-minute roasting time for a whole chicken, quartered. You may find that you like your vegetables cooked a little more or a little less than I do, and I can think of nothing cooler than for people to write notes into a cookbook I've written, so use this chart as a jumping-off point. I am going to roast so many vegetables for dinner tonight!

Add after
5 MINUTES . . .

Beet

Onion

Potato

Sweet potato

Total cooking time:
60 minutes

Add after
15 MINUTES . . .

Carrot

Celery root

Squash

Turnip

Total cooking time:
50 minutes

Add after
30 MINUTES . . .

Cabbage

Cauliflower

Fennel

Romanesco

Total cooking time:
35 minutes

Add after
40 MINUTES . . .

Cherry tomatoes

Corn kernels

Mung bean sprouts

Zucchini

Total cooking time:
25 minutes

Add after
45 MINUTES . . .

Asparagus

Bell pepper

Broccoli

Mushrooms

Total cooking time:
20 minutes

Add after
1 HOUR . . .

Arugula, spinach,
or baby kale

Peas

Sugar snap peas

Total cooking time:
5 minutes

Chicken Meatloaf with Peppery Glaze & Cabbage Slaw

Serves 4 to 6 (or makes 6 to 8 cold meatloaf sandwiches)

Cabbage Slaw

½ head green cabbage

3 tablespoons freshly squeezed lemon juice

1 tablespoon extra-virgin olive oil

1 teaspoon kosher salt

½ cup (20g) chopped cilantro

Meatloaf

2 garlic cloves

½ head green cabbage

¼ large yellow onion

1 pound (450g) ground chicken, or 1¼ pounds (570g) boneless, skinless chicken thighs, for grinding

½ cup (55g) fine bread crumbs

1 large egg, beaten

1 tablespoon rice wine vinegar

1½ teaspoons kosher salt

¼ teaspoon dried oregano

¼ teaspoon ground coriander

Peppery Glaze

2 tablespoons ketchup

½ tablespoon gochujang

½ tablespoon honey

¼ teaspoon dried oregano

¼ teaspoon garlic powder

Oh hi, I didn't see you there. I was just making this chicken meatloaf while watching the 2005 movie adaptation of *Pride and Prejudice* starring Keira Knightley and drinking a glass of unfiltered rosé as the sun sets. (Haven't you ever wanted to say that to somebody?!) This meatloaf is easy to throw together and makes for a pretty perfect meal—especially with the spicy, sour, sweet glaze that goes on top. It's like a classic ketchup-Worcestershire meatloaf glaze, with tons more umami and a kick from the gochujang (Korean fermented chile paste), and it works so well with the lean, mild chicken and crunchy cabbage slaw! If you don't finish all the meatloaf for dinner, you can use leftovers for cold meatloaf sandwiches with slaw and mustard.

1. To make the slaw, shred the cabbage in a food processor with the slicer attachment, or chop by hand into matchsticks about ⅛ inch (3mm) thick. In a large mixing bowl, combine the lemon juice, oil, salt, and cilantro and mix well. Transfer the shredded cabbage to the mixing bowl and toss with the dressing.

2. To make the meatloaf, heat the oven to 350°F (175°C). Put the standard blade back in the food processor and add the garlic, cabbage, and onion and process until finely chopped (you can also do this by hand). Transfer to a mixing bowl. If you're grinding the chicken yourself, first cut the meat into even 1-inch (2.5cm) pieces. Working in small batches, place the chicken in the processor and pulse to finely chop, but avoid turning it into a mousse. Add the chicken to the cabbage mixture, then add the bread crumbs, egg, vinegar, salt, oregano, and coriander and mix. Grease a half sheet pan with oil or cooking spray and transfer the chicken mixture to it, forming it into a log shape about 12 by 4 inches (30 by 10cm).

3. To make the glaze, in a small bowl, whisk together the ketchup, gochujang, honey, oregano, and garlic powder. Pour the glaze over the meatloaf and use a pastry brush or silicone spatula to spread it evenly over the top.

4. Bake the meatloaf for 45 minutes to 1 hour, until it's cooked through and the internal temperature is 150°F (65°C). Let the meatloaf rest for 15 minutes or so before slicing and serving it with the slaw.

Lemongrass-Poached Chicken Legs with Sugar Snap Peas

Serves 4

8 cups (1.9L) water

1 medium onion, thinly sliced

4 lemongrass stalks, cut in a few pieces

6 garlic cloves, smashed

2 whole cloves

½ tablespoon kosher salt

4 whole chicken legs (thighs and drumsticks), about 3 pounds (1.4kg)

Lemongrass Velouté

3 tablespoons unsalted butter

3 tablespoons all-purpose flour

1½ teaspoons freshly squeezed lemon juice

Pinch of kosher salt

1 pound (450g) sugar snap peas, stems and strings removed (split lengthwise if you're feeling fancy)

1 teaspoon kosher salt

1 teaspoon extra-virgin olive oil

Poaching chicken in a simple lemongrass broth will make your home smell like chicken soup and Froot Loops in a nice way, and we could just stop there and eat ridiculously tender chicken and sip on a flavorful broth. But velouté is my favorite of the French mother sauces, made by thickening a light stock (traditionally chicken, fish, or veal) with a light roux, so why wouldn't we do that here? After the chicken poaches, we'll turn the poaching liquid into a velouté, and broil the chicken with some snap peas to crisp the skin and render the peas helplessly delicious. You'll need a fair amount of liquid to keep the chicken submerged, so this recipe makes plenty of sauce, which a nice loaf of bread can help you take care of.

1. In a large saucepan, combine the water, onion, lemongrass, garlic, cloves, and the ½ tablespoon salt. Submerge the chicken legs in the liquid. Bring the liquid to a boil over high heat, turn the heat to medium-low, and simmer for 20 to 30 minutes, until the chicken is firm to the touch and the skin of the drumstick is starting to pull back from the bone. Transfer the chicken to a platter and let the skin air-dry while you make the velouté. Strain the poaching liquid through a medium-mesh sieve and set aside.

2. To make the velouté, melt the butter in a small saucepan over medium heat. Add the flour and whisk until completely combined. Cook for about 2 minutes, stirring regularly, until the mixture smells like toasty butter but the flour has not begun to brown. Slowly pour 2 cups (480ml) of the poaching liquid into the roux, whisking constantly to prevent lumps. It will steam and hiss aggressively, which is why you're not supposed to mix hot liquid with hot roux, but you're a rebel and a very cautious one at that, so I am not worried about you. Turn the heat to high and bring the sauce to a boil, whisking constantly. Add the lemon juice and a pinch of salt.

3. Heat the broiler. In a small mixing bowl, toss the snap peas with the 1 teaspoon salt and the oil. Spread them out on a half sheet pan or roasting pan and add the chicken legs, skin-side up. Put the pan under the broiler and broil for 5 minutes, until the chicken skin is brown and bubbly and the snap peas are dark around the edges but still nice and green.

4. Divide the chicken legs and snap peas into four shallow bowls, ladle some velouté over each, and serve.

Stewy Chicken with Eggplant & Mint

Serves 8

3 tablespoons
vegetable oil

1 eggplant, peeled and cut
into 1-inch (2.5cm) chunks
(about 4 cups)

8 garlic cloves, smashed

One 15-ounce (425g)
can chickpeas, drained,
liquid reserved

1½ ounces (40g) okra,
stems removed, cut into
¼-inch (6mm) rounds
(about ⅓ cup)

1 pound (450g) boneless,
skinless chicken breasts or
thighs, sliced lengthwise
into ¼-inch (6mm) strips

1½ cups (355ml)
chicken stock (see page 9)

1 tablespoon molasses

½ tablespoon kosher salt

½ cup (20g) mint leaves

Cooked rice, for serving

In this quick and easy stew, we'll stretch a pound of chicken to feed a small army. By slicing it thin, combining it with satisfying hearty vegetables, and serving it with a big pot of rice, we'll get a ton of delicious food for about $1 per person. Here, boneless, skinless chicken (breast or thigh) is cooked with eggplant, which we'll peel and dice to prevent any sponginess or toughness from the skin; chickpeas, half of which we'll smash to add some texture and heft to the stew; okra, which I know people sometimes avoid because they think it's too slimy, but when you simmer okra in broth, the extra slime acts as another thickener; and mint, which makes everything taste like summertime, and I love summertime. We'll flavor it all with chicken stock (page 9) and a hefty amount of garlic, but feel free to toast a pinch or two of spices like crushed pink peppercorns, fennel seeds, or paprika in the pan before adding in the eggplant. I think this stew is pretty awesome over cooked rice.

1. In a large saucepan or Dutch oven, heat 2 tablespoons of the oil over high heat until smoking. Add the eggplant and cook undisturbed until nicely caramelized on one side, about 5 minutes. Stir and continue cooking, lowering the heat if the eggplant starts to get too charred, for another 7 to 10 minutes, or until you have some color all over the eggplant chunks. Add the garlic and the remaining 1 tablespoon oil and cook for another minute, or until the garlic is fragrant and nicely caramelized.

2. In a small mixing bowl, smash half of the chickpeas into a thick but consistent paste, using the reserved liquid to moisten as needed. Add the paste to the pan with the eggplant, then add the okra, remaining whole chickpeas, chicken, stock, molasses, and salt and bring the whole mixture to a boil, stirring frequently. Lower the heat and simmer until the chicken is no longer pink, 3 to 5 minutes. Turn off the heat, add the mint, and stir to combine. Serve over cooked rice.

Chicken Thighs with Mushrooms & Riesling

Serves 4

1 tablespoon extra-virgin olive oil

4 bone-in, skin-on chicken thighs, about 1½ pounds (680g)

1 tablespoon kosher salt

1 tablespoon all-purpose flour

¾ pound (340g) mushrooms, any variety, sliced

5 garlic cloves, finely minced

¼ teaspoon ground cardamom

¼ teaspoon ground coriander

1½ cups (355ml) Riesling

½ cup (120ml) chicken stock

1 tablespoon unsalted butter

½ cup (20g) chopped fresh herbs (such as dill, mint, basil, parsley, or a mix)

½ bunch scallions, white and green parts, thinly sliced

Cooked pasta, cooked rice, or bread, for serving

Seriously, this dish is winey and buttery and comforting and faintly reminds me of chicken marsala, and who doesn't love chicken marsala? You can use whatever mushrooms you like; I like a mix of button (my go-to cheap, delicious utility mushroom), shiitake (not my all-time favorite mushroom, texture-wise, but definitely the most flavorful), and maitake (aka hen of the woods, for even more texture), but honestly any other varieties would be great! And you could use a wine other than Riesling, but I love the complexity and almost floral sweetness it brings, which balances nicely with the warm spices in the dish. Yes, I know, it is entirely uncool to like white wine that isn't super dry, but I'm not sure why, and we don't have to live our lives the way other people want us to just to be polite.

1. Heat the oil in a large sauté pan with high sides over high heat until smoking. Season the chicken thighs with the salt and add them to the pan, skin-side down. Lower the heat a little so that they don't burn, and cook until the skin is nicely caramelized, 10 to 12 minutes. Transfer the chicken to a plate.

2. To the pan, add the flour and cook, stirring constantly, for 3 to 5 minutes, until lightly browned. Add the mushrooms and give everything a stir, cooking for another 1 to 2 minutes and accepting that it would take too long to completely brown the mushrooms and they taste just as good when they're not fully browned. Add the garlic, cardamom, and coriander and mix to combine. Add the wine and stock, stirring continuously until no lumps of toasted flour remain. Add the chicken thighs back into the pan, skin-side up, and nestle them in the liquid. Bring to a boil and continue to boil until the liquid has reduced by half, 15 to 20 minutes.

3. Turn off the heat and mix in the butter, herbs, and scallions. This is delicious served over pasta or rice, or just with some nice crusty bread to soak up the sauce.

Cider-Braised Drumsticks with Bacon, Fennel & Apples

Serves 4

4 ounces (115g) bacon, sliced into 2-inch (5cm) pieces

8 chicken drumsticks, about 2 pounds (900g)

4 garlic cloves, smashed

½ small fennel bulb, cored and thinly sliced

2 Gala apples, peeled and sliced into ½-inch (1.3cm) wedges

1 teaspoon kosher salt

1 cup (240ml) hard cider (look for a sweet or semisweet kind)

Roasted potatoes, for serving

I pretty much always want something braised for dinner, and as much as I love braising the legs of a cow, pig, or lamb, they take a few hours to get tender and thus aren't always the best option for a weeknight. A chicken's legs, on the other hand, braise in less than an hour, so you can have a righteous braised dish any night of the stupid week! This super simple stew is inspired by autumn flavors, using bacon, fennel, and apples (both fresh and in hard apple cider). You could totally swap out the hard cider if you're not into the alcohol, but I would use chicken stock or water rather than apple juice or fresh cider, either of which would make it a little too sweet. There's something about the smoky, salty, sweet, and slightly bitter elements of this dish, cooked down with chicken that is just starting to fall apart, that makes me want to smoke cigars and write a novel, but I don't actually like cigars, and if I wrote a novel, it would just be a fictional cookbook, so it's probably better to stick with cooking chicken for now.

1. Heat the oven to 400°F (200°C).

2. In a small sauté pan over medium heat, cook the bacon until brown and a little crispy, 7 to 10 minutes. Remove the bacon from the pan with a slotted spoon and set aside on a plate.

3. Pour the remaining bacon fat into a large ovenproof sauté pan or Dutch oven and put it on the stove over medium-high heat. (We are using a fresh pan to prevent the chicken skin from sticking to the bottom while crisping up, which is annoying.) When the fat starts to smoke, add the drumsticks and cook until nicely browned on all sides, about 5 minutes per side.

4. Add the garlic to the pan and cook until lightly browned and fragrant, 3 to 5 minutes. Add the bacon, fennel, apples, and salt and give everything a good stir. Continue cooking on high heat for 5 minutes more, until the fennel is looking translucent and is soft to the touch, and the apples start to caramelize. Add the cider, scrape the bottom of the pan to deglaze, bring the mixture to a boil, turn off the heat, and transfer the pan to the oven, uncovered.

5. Cook the chicken and vegetables for 50 to 60 minutes, or until the top of the chicken looks dark and the liquid has reduced by half. Really, you could pull it out after 30 minutes (or as soon as the chicken is 165°F/75°C), but I like my drumsticks to be falling apart. Serve with roasted potatoes alongside.

Parmesan-Sake Grilled Chicken

Serves 4

2 ounces (55g) Parmesan, shredded

½ cup (120ml) dry sake

6 garlic cloves

1 tablespoon kosher salt, plus 2 teaspoons

1 tablespoon distilled white vinegar

4 split (bone-in, skin-on) chicken breasts, about 3 pounds (1.4kg)

1 pound (450g) broccolini

2 teaspoons extra-virgin olive oil

Onion Gravy

1 tablespoon extra-virgin olive oil

1 medium yellow onion, sliced ½-inch (1.3cm) thick

1 teaspoon kosher salt

1 tablespoon dry sake

1 tablespoon distilled white vinegar

1 teaspoon cornstarch

1 cup (240ml) chicken stock

I love the flavor of chicken so much. So when I marinate it, I'm not looking to overwhelm that flavor but enhance it. I like to pack the marinade with always-flavor-enhancing umami, using one of the most umami-forward ingredients of them all: Parmesan cheese. You might ask, what happens when you puree Parmesan with sake and garlic, soak chicken breasts in that mixture, and grill them? Awesome things! When I did it, the chicken got charred and super caramelized (yours might get really dark in some spots, and maybe even have rad grill marks—no matter what, it will taste great), and now I want to make a smoky sake and Parmesan sauce to put on chicken sandwiches and in my hair.

1. Combine the Parmesan, sake, garlic, the 1 tablespoon salt, and the vinegar in a blender and puree until smooth. Put the chicken in a ziplock freezer bag and pour in the marinade, then seal the bag and shake well. Put the bag in a bowl or plastic container and refrigerate for 12 to 24 hours.

2. Heat the grill to July 10th, 1913, Death Valley, California, or as hot as it will go, leaving a cooler region on the grill (if using charcoal, push it all to one side of the grill so there is an area without charcoal underneath; on a gas grill, turn one burner way down). Pat the chicken skin dry and oil the grill. Place the chicken on the grate, skin-side down, and grill for 30 to 40 minutes, flipping occasionally and keeping in mind that the bone side needs more time than the skin side. If it's getting too dark, move it to the grill's cooler region. The chicken is done when it has an internal temperature of 155°F (70°C). Set the chicken aside on a plate and tent some aluminum foil over it to help keep it warm.

3. While the grill is still hot, combine the broccolini, oil, and the remaining 2 teaspoons salt in a small mixing bowl and mix well. Spread the broccolini out on the grill, perpendicular to the grate, and cook until lightly charred but still crunchy, 7 to 10 minutes.

4. To make the gravy, heat the oil in a small saucepan over high heat. Add the onion and salt and cook, stirring regularly, until the onion is lightly caramelized and smells amazing, about 10 minutes. In a bowl or measuring cup, whisk the sake, vinegar, and cornstarch into the chicken stock. Pour the mixture into the saucepan with the onion, stirring constantly. Bring the gravy to a boil and remove from the heat.

5. Serve the chicken with the broccolini and gravy if you love your family!

Meyer Lemon Chicken Salad Sandwiches

Makes enough for at least 6 sandwiches

¼ cup (60g) strained Greek yogurt

¼ cup (60ml) freshly squeezed Meyer lemon juice

1 tablespoon Meyer lemon zest

2 tablespoons Kewpie mayonnaise

¼ small red cabbage, chopped into ¼-inch (6mm) pieces

¼ red onion, diced

1 teaspoon kosher salt

2½ cups (350g) shredded cooked chicken

12 slices toasted rye bread

12 slices avocado

12 slices cooked bacon

Freshly ground black pepper

Meyer lemons are so fun and special. They're really only around in the winter, when everything is sad and dark, but then a bright, golden Meyer lemon shows up smelling like a cross between a lemon, an orange, and an Everlasting Gobstopper. They're not always the easiest to find, but when you see them, buy them—and you won't be disappointed! Meyer lemons are super juicy, and if they're on the larger size, a single lemon is all you need to make this recipe. The juice is delicious, less tart than a regular lemon, but the zest is what's really extraordinary—and here you'll use both. (If you can't find them, just use a combination of regular lemon and orange juice and zest.) This salad is an excellent way to repurpose leftover chicken, like from Szechuan Pepper–Lacquered Chicken (page 74) or Chicken Pot-au-Feu (page 91), or you can roast 2 to 3 boneless, skinless chicken breasts or thighs (½ to ¾ pounds, 340 to 510g; see page 7) for the dish. I use red cabbage to add crunch and because it makes the salad look amazing and it won't overpower the Meyer lemon.

1. In a large mixing bowl, combine the yogurt, lemon juice, lemon zest, mayo, cabbage, onion, and salt and mix thoroughly. Add the chicken and stir to combine.

2. Divide the chicken salad among six slices of the bread. Top with two slices of avocado and two slices of bacon each, then sprinkle with a pinch of cracked black pepper. Top each with the remaining slices of bread and serve.

Speedy Chicken Chili

Serves 6 to 8

1 ounce (30g) dried guajillo chiles, stems and seeds removed

1 ounce (30g) dried ancho chiles, stems and seeds removed

3 tablespoons vegetable oil

1 yellow onion, chopped into ½-inch (1.3cm) cubes

6 garlic cloves, smashed

1 tablespoon kosher salt

1 teaspoon whole cumin seeds

¼ teaspoon dried sage

¼ teaspoon dried thyme

¼ teaspoon dried rosemary

¼ teaspoon dried marjoram

4 cups (950ml) chicken stock

2 chipotle chiles in adobo sauce

2 tablespoons rice wine vinegar

1 tablespoon light brown sugar

¼ teaspoon freshly ground black pepper

Pinch of grated nutmeg

3 pounds (1.4kg) boneless, skinless chicken thighs

When I worked for a chef from Texas (whose fried chicken recipe is on page 61), I learned about all of the things that do not belong in chili. Patrick Farrell gave me the impression that if it has much more than meat and dried chiles, then it's not really chili. To honor Patrick, I did not put a single bean in this recipe, but I did put a lot of chicken in it, so he and the entire state of Texas will probably be upset anyway. This version is quick and simple to make: Stew some relatively mild guajillo and ancho chiles, puree them into a sauce, and cook chopped chicken in that sauce. I've included suggestions for fun toppings on the opposite page—try the corn and scallion salad, crushed tortilla chips, and sour cream, or serve with any combination of chopped raw onions, pickled onions, shredded Cheddar cheese, or adorable oyster crackers. I won't officially recommend serving it over spaghetti, like they do in Cincinnati, because Patrick will be even more upset (though he will never know if you do, and my Ohioan buddy, Keith, would be thrilled!).

1. In a dry sauté pan, toast the dried chiles over medium heat until super fragrant, 3 to 4 minutes. Set aside. To a saucepan over medium-high heat, add 1 tablespoon of the oil, along with the onion, garlic, salt, cumin, sage, thyme, rosemary, and marjoram and cook, stirring, until the onion softens, about 5 minutes. Add the stock, chipotles and sauce, vinegar, brown sugar, toasted dried chiles, pepper, and nutmeg. Stir and bring this to a boil, turn the heat to medium-low, and simmer until the chiles are fully hydrated and the onion is translucent. Remove the mixture from the heat, transfer it to a blender, letting some steam escape, and puree until very smooth.

2. Chop the chicken into ¼-inch (6mm) cubes, or cube into 1-inch (2.5cm) pieces and process in a food processor until the pieces are roughly ¼ inch (6mm). You want it a little chunkier than ground chicken.

3. In a large stockpot, heat the remaining 2 tablespoons oil over high heat and add the chopped chicken in one large block. Cook the chicken until nicely caramelized, 7 to 10 minutes. Flip the block of chicken (don't worry if it breaks up a little), and cook it on the other side for 7 to 10 minutes, until also caramelized. Turn off the heat and stir to slightly cool. Add the pureed chiles and combine everything well, bring to a boil over high heat, then lower the heat and simmer for 30 minutes, until the chicken is tender and the sauce has reached a thick, spoonable consistency.

4. Serve by itself or with any of the suggested toppings.

Soft-Boiled Eggs

In a 2-quart (1.9L) saucepan over high heat, bring water to a boil. Gently drop in as many eggs as you have bowls of chili and cook for 6½ minutes. Transfer the eggs to an ice bath, chill just long enough so that you can handle them, then peel the eggs and serve them on top of the chili.

Corn & Scallion Salad

In a mixing bowl, combine 2 cups (250g) cooked corn kernels with ½ cup (60g) chopped scallions (white and green parts), 2 teaspoons distilled white vinegar, 1 teaspoon extra-virgin olive oil, and ½ teaspoon kosher salt. Mix well to combine and serve on top of the chili.

Broiled Jalapeños

Heat the broiler to the highest setting. Toss 4 whole jalapeños with ½ teaspoon extra-virgin olive oil and ¼ teaspoon kosher salt and broil on a sheet pan until nicely charred on one side, about 4 minutes. Once they're cool enough to handle, slice the jalapeños and use as a garnish for the chili.

WEEKNIGHT CHICKEN DINNER MATRIX

Dinner should never be stressful—it's your reward for surviving another day! But sometimes it's hard to figure out what to make, and you don't want to spend all night working on it, but you also don't want to play *Chopped* while staring into your refrigerator deciding what to do. I get it and I am here for you. Below are some fun and easy ideas to get you started. Just prep your chicken in a style from the first column, pick a flavor bonus to give it some oomph, and finish off your plate with a quick veg side and a fun sauce. Mix and match to put together a combo that sounds fun—or just use this as inspiration. And then commit, pour yourself a drink, put on the classical radio station, and enjoy cooking!

CHICKEN PREP	FLAVOR BONUSES	QUICK VEGETABLE SIDES	SAUCES
Pounded and grilled breasts (see page 20)	Gochujang or miso rub	Sautéed zucchini (see page 23)	Scallion-horseradish sauce (see page 91)
Schnitzel (see page 16)	Ras el hanout rub	Grilled broccolini (page 48)	Chicken stock gravy (see page 98)
Poached legs (see page 40)	Italian dressing marinade	Sweet potato wedges (see page 127)	Lemongrass velouté (see page 40)
Broiled thighs (see page 15)	Thyme/oregano/ rosemary, minced	Herby rice noodle salad (see page 83)	Pecan romesco sauce (see page 101)
Roasted quarters (see page 35)	Parmesan-sake marinade (see page 48)	Braised greens (see page 116)	Apricot-basil puree (see page 101)

A FEW FAVORITE COMBOS

Pounded and grilled breasts + oregano coating + sautéed zucchini + lemongrass velouté

Schnitzel + rosemary coating + grilled broccolini + apricot-basil puree

Roasted quarters + gochujang/miso rub + sweet potato wedges + chicken stock gravy

Poached legs + thyme in poaching liquid + braised greens + scallion-horseradish sauce

Broiled thighs + Parmesan-sake marinade + herby rice noodle salad + pecan romesco sauce

Big, Arduous, Fulfilling Projects

Pepperoni Spiced–Chicken Pizza

Makes 2 small pizzas, which serves 4

New York City–Style Pizza Dough, aka the Best Pizza Dough in the World

3½ cups (440g) King Arthur bread flour, plus more for dusting

½ tablespoon kosher salt

¾ teaspoon instant yeast

1¼ cups (300ml) water

Pepperoni-Spiced Chicken

1 teaspoon yellow mustard seeds

1 teaspoon fennel seeds

1 small star anise

¼ teaspoon black peppercorns

¼ teaspoon red pepper flakes

¼ teaspoon smoked paprika

4 bone-in chicken thighs, about 1½ pounds (680g), skin removed

3 garlic cloves, finely minced

1 teaspoon low-sodium soy sauce

1 teaspoon extra-virgin olive oil

½ teaspoon kosher salt

First thing: This will not be a popular opinion, but I find that porky, salty, spicy pepperoni somewhat clashes with an otherwise perfect slice of pizza. That said, flavoring *chicken* with perfectly amazing pepperoni spices and putting it on pizza makes for a leaner, mellower, better balanced slice. And I realize that with that sentence you may have thrown this book in a blazing-hot oven. But if you're still here, know that you will not fool anybody into thinking the chicken is actually pepperoni, but why are you trying to trick your friends anyway? Just be honest with them and enjoy this pie—which has a tender, chewy crust, melty cheese, and lots of perfectly cooked chicken.

Second thing: I think you really have to just give up and applaud the photo to the right. Somehow, someone cut this pizza into an odd number of slices without even dirtying the pizza cutter and I would apologize except that it's so amazing and I can't stop staring at it. But seriously, who cut this pizza?!

1. Make the dough first; it needs a minimum of 4 hours to rise, and ideally 8 hours (you can skip the second rise if need be). Put the flour, salt, and yeast in a food processor and pulse it a couple of times to mix. Add the water and process until a ball forms and whips around the edge of the bowl for about 30 seconds. Turn the dough out onto the counter dusted with a little flour, knead it for 5 to 10 minutes, until it's no longer sticky. Do not be bummed if your dough looks shaggy and not smooth like professional pizza dough. It will—it just needs to relax so the flour can fully hydrate. Put the dough in a bowl, cover with plastic wrap, and let it sit at room temperature for 4 hours.

2. After 4 hours, scrape the dough out of the bowl and check out how amazing it feels! Weigh the dough and cut it in half, making sure that each half is about 365g. (If you don't have a scale, just eyeball it. And if you bought dough at the store *and* don't own a scale, the dough should be roughly baseball-size.) Roll the balls on the counter to round them, put each on a separate plate, and cover each with a large inverted bowl; this will make it easier to eventually scoop up the dough without squishing out all of the air. Let the dough balls rise for another 4 hours while you prep the rest of the ingredients. By then they should have doubled in size, with a bubble or two puffing up.

CONTINUED

Pizza Sauce

1 cup (250g) crushed tomatoes

¼ teaspoon kosher salt

To Assemble

1 cup (110g) shredded low-moisture mozzarella

¼ red onion, thinly sliced into rounds

Handful of fresh parsley or basil leaves (optional)

Grated Parmesan (optional)

3. Heat the oven to 400°F (200°C), with your pizza stone (or a rimless inverted sheet pan) on a rack. I like to place mine near the broiler (which we'll use at the end).

4. Let's cook chicken! In a blender or spice grinder, add the mustard seeds, fennel seeds, star anise, peppercorns, red pepper flakes, and smoked paprika and grind into a fine powder. Transfer the spices to a medium mixing bowl and add the chicken thighs, garlic, soy sauce, oil, and salt and mix well. Place the thighs on a sheet pan and put the pan in the oven, directly on the baking stone, to use the direct heat the stone has absorbed. Cook the chicken for 45 minutes, or until it is no longer pink and the meat pulls away from the bone. Once it has cooled enough to handle, shred it and reserve.

5. Increase the oven temperature to as high as it will go, with the pizza stone still inside—for most standard ovens, this will be 500°F (260°C). (The hotter the stone, the bubblier the crust.)

6. To make the super simple sauce, mix the tomatoes with the salt in a bowl.

7. Dust your pizza peel (or a wooden cutting board or inverted sheet pan) with a little flour and set it aside. Then, stretch out the dough. The main objectives here are to keep the shape round and not knock the air out of the edges. With one dough ball on a well-floured counter, define the outer crust with your fingertips by pressing a ring into the dough about an inch from the edge all the way around. Using that lip as a guide, stretch the dough with your hands, pulling on the edge and not worrying about the middle until you can pick up the dough and fit it over your hands. Continue to stretch the dough from the middle outward, letting the rest hang off of your hands until it is uniform in width and about 14 inches (36cm) in diameter. Lay the stretched dough on top of the pizza peel.

8. Spread half of the sauce on the dough and follow with half of the mozzarella, half of the chicken, and some red onion. Slide the pizza off of the peel and onto the heated pizza stone by shimmying an edge of the pie onto the stone and gently but confidently pulling the peel away. Depending on how serious your oven is, bake the pizza for 4 to 8 minutes, until the bottom is nice and browned and the cheese is bubbling. If the top is too pale and the bottom is dark enough, turn on the broiler to get a little more color.

9. Pull the pizza out of the oven, sprinkle with a little parsley or basil and Parmesan (if using), and let it rest before slicing while you make the other one.

Patrick's Fried Chicken with Spicy Pickles

Serves 4

Pickles

2 large cucumbers, cut into ¼-inch (6mm) slices

1 cup (240ml) distilled white vinegar

2 scallions, white and green parts, thinly sliced

1 shallot, finely chopped

1 tablespoon granulated sugar

One 1-inch (2.5cm) piece ginger, peeled and minced

1 garlic clove, minced

¼ to 1 teaspoon red pepper flakes

¼ teaspoon toasted sesame oil

Fried Chicken

1½ cups (190g) all-purpose flour

1 tablespoon kosher salt

½ teaspoon coarsely ground black pepper

1 egg

1 cup (240ml) whole milk

One 3- to 4-pound (1.4 to 1.8kg) chicken, cut into 10 pieces (see page 4)

6 cups (1.4L) vegetable or canola oil, for frying

Hot Maple

1 cup (240ml) maple syrup

1 tablespoon red pepper flakes

My friend, chef Patrick Farrell, is happy to teach anybody everything he knows about food. He taught me a lot of what I now know about cooking, and working for him was one of the most important parts of my culinary education. That said, he flat-out refused to teach me how to make his fried chicken. As I've said, he is a proud Texan who hopes to someday open up a fried chicken shop, and believes this secret recipe will pay for his retirement. For years, I had to casually pretend not to watch while he butchered, seasoned, breaded, and fried his birds, until eventually I figured it out on my own—the key is really in its simple perfection, which creates a crunchy-but-not-too-crunchy crust that's almost like the edges of a good biscuit. Patrick is going to hate me when he sees his secret recipe in a cookbook, but we will drink a beer together and he will forgive me.

I like to serve pickles with Patrick's fried chicken, for some salty tartness to complement the crispy stuff. The ones here are my own adaptation of *oi muchim*, a Korean cucumber salad, with spicy ginger and red pepper flakes to add some brightness to the chicken and to the hot maple syrup we'll drizzle all over the top.

1. To make the pickles, in a large mixing bowl, stir together the cucumbers, vinegar, scallions, shallot, sugar, ginger, garlic, red pepper flakes, and sesame oil until fully mixed. Transfer to a nonreactive container with a lid, cover, and refrigerate for at least 1 hour or up to the rest of your life (not really— just 2 weeks or so would be fine).

2. To make the chicken, meanwhile, in a large bowl, stir together the flour, 2½ teaspoons of the salt, and the black pepper until well mixed.

3. In a small bowl, crack the egg and whisk until beaten. Place 1 tablespoon of the beaten egg in a separate large bowl, discarding the rest. To this, add the milk and the remaining ½ teaspoon salt and whisk to combine.

4. Working with one piece of chicken at a time, toss the chicken in the seasoned flour to completely coat it. Dip into the milk-egg mixture, then dredge it once again in the flour, making sure it's completely coated. Put the chicken on a plate and repeat with the remaining pieces.

CONTINUED

5. Pour the vegetable oil into a 3-quart (2.8L) or larger saucepan for frying. The oil should come only halfway up the sides of the pan, so when it expands with the heat and then bubbles up with the addition of chicken, there is plenty of room for the oil in the pan and it won't spatter onto your stove. Heat the oil over high heat to 325° to 350°F (165° to 175°C), measuring the temperature with a candy or fryer thermometer (or your animal instincts), and then turn the heat to low.

6. Fry the chicken in two batches so that the chicken isn't crowded in the pot. Gently place half of the chicken in the oil. Fry the chicken for about 10 minutes, flipping regularly (especially if the chicken is not completely submerged, which is totally fine!), until it is golden brown on the outside and not at all pink on the inside. As you are frying the chicken, increase the heat as needed to maintain the temperature at 325° to 350°F (165° to 175°C). Remove with a slotted spoon and drain on a wire rack or on paper towels. Fry the second batch.

7. While the chicken is frying, make the hot maple by combining the maple syrup and red pepper flakes in a blender and pureeing until smooth. This will be pretty spicy but also super sweet—a little will go a long way. (For a milder flavor, decrease the red pepper flakes to ½ teaspoon or even ¼ teaspoon.)

8. Place the chicken on a plate, spread some pickles around it, drizzle everything with a little bit of the hot maple, and serve.

Chicken & Grits Tamales with Salsa Más Macha

Makes 16 tamales with a lot of extra salsa

Salsa Más Macha

½ cup (120ml) vegetable oil

½ cup (70g) raw, unsalted sunflower seeds

2 tablespoons sesame seeds

8 garlic cloves, smashed

6 guajillo or ancho chiles, stems and seeds removed

1 chipotle chile in adobo sauce

½ cup (120ml) distilled white vinegar

¼ cup (60ml) freshly squeezed lemon juice

2 tablespoons maple syrup

1 teaspoon kosher salt

Tamales

16 dried corn husks, plus 1 additional husk, torn into thin strips, lengthwise, for tying

10 cups (2.4L) chicken stock

4 cups (760g) grits

1 tablespoon kosher salt

6 cups (750g) shredded cooked chicken (see page 7)

One of my cooks often brings in magnificent tamales that he buys near his apartment, my favorite of which has chicken and mole. And they're all made with masa harina—finely ground cornmeal treated with slaked lime that requires only cold water to soften it—cooked with stock, fat, and plenty of salt. Like grits! Grits are also made with cornmeal, but it's coarsely ground, untreated, and needs to be boiled. I tried making chicken tamales with chicken-stock grits because that is how my stupid mind works. The salsa más macha here—a sauce from Veracruz, Mexico, with dried chiles, garlic, nuts or seeds, oil, and vinegar—is a super-strong combination of Alex Stupak's in *Tacos: Recipes and Provocations*, Zarela Martinez's in *Zarela's Veracruz: Mexico's Simplest Cuisine*, and EmilyC's from Food52.

1. To make the salsa, combine the oil, sunflower seeds, sesame seeds, and garlic in a saucepan and cook over medium heat until the seeds are golden brown, about 7 minutes. Add the dried chiles and the chipotle with sauce, turn off the heat, and let the mixture steep for 10 minutes. Transfer to a blender; add the vinegar, lemon juice, maple syrup, and salt; and puree until smooth. Transfer to a bowl and chill completely.

2. To make the tamales, soak the corn husks in warm water for 20 minutes. Meanwhile, in a saucepan over high heat, bring the stock to a boil. Whisk in the grits and the salt. Turn the heat to medium-low and cook until the grits have fully absorbed the stock, about 20 minutes.

3. In a sauté pan over medium heat, combine the shredded chicken and 1 cup (240ml) of the salsa and heat through.

4. Lay out a soaked corn husk and spread some grits in the middle of it, leaving a 2-inch (5cm) border around the edges. Add 1 tablespoon of chicken on top of the grits, then fold up the bottom of the husk and tuck in the sides, leaving the top open. Tie the tamale closed with a thin strip of husk. Repeat with the remaining husks.

5. Set up a steamer in a lidded stockpot large enough to fit 8 tamales standing up. Add about ½ inch (1.3cm) of water. Place the tamales upright, open-end up, leaning them against the side of the pot. Bring the water to a boil over high heat, cover, turn the heat to low, and steam for about 25 minutes, until warmed through. Repeat with the second batch of tamales. Serve with lots of salsa.

Chicken & Sesame Dumplings in Miso Broth

Serves 6 to 8

Miso Broth

1 teaspoon vegetable oil

4 bone-in, skin-on chicken thighs, about 1½ pounds (680g)

2 carrots, chopped into 1-inch-thick (2.5cm-thick) slices on the bias

½ yellow onion, chopped into ¼-inch (6mm) pieces

8 cups (1.9L) chicken stock

½ cup (140g) white miso

½ teaspoon kosher salt

Sesame Dumplings

2 cups (250g) all-purpose flour

1 tablespoon baking powder

1 tablespoon black sesame seeds

1 teaspoon kosher salt

1 teaspoon garlic powder

1 cup (240ml) whole milk

2 tablespoons unsalted butter, melted

2 tablespoons tahini

¼ teaspoon toasted sesame oil

To Serve

½ head radicchio, shredded super thin

½ cup (10g) cilantro leaves

2 limes, cut in wedges

I love using miso to flavor things. But if you're thinking that this dish will taste like miso soup with Southern-style dumplings in it, you'll find something else entirely. By simmering the miso in chicken stock with mirepoix, you'll see another, gentler side of it, and the big, fluffy dumplings flavored with sesame in three forms—seeds, paste, and oil—add tons of earthiness. You might be surprised by how huge the dumplings get, like a significantly more delicious version of those little pills you soak in water that turn out to be sponges shaped like dinosaurs. This recipe is in the Big, Arduous, Fulfilling Projects chapter because it is all of those things, especially if you don't have stock on hand. But if you have stock and leftover shredded chicken, then this can actually be a 30-minute gateway to a fulfilling project that you can make any night of the week!

1. To make the broth, in a large stockpot, heat the vegetable oil over high heat until smoking. Add the chicken thighs, skin-side down, and cook until they're nicely browned, about 5 minutes. Flip and cook on the other side for 5 minutes. Pour out all but 1 tablespoon of fat from the pot, add the carrots and onion, and cook, stirring, until the vegetables start to caramelize and smell amazing, 5 minutes. Add the stock, miso, and salt; bring to a boil; and turn the heat to low. Simmer for 45 minutes, or until the meat is very tender and is falling off the bone.

2. While the chicken is cooking, make the dumplings. In a large mixing bowl, combine the flour, baking powder, sesame seeds, salt, and garlic powder and mix well. Add the milk, butter, tahini, and sesame oil and stir to combine, but don't go too crazy because we don't want it to get too glutinous. The dough should look pretty uniform but not totally smooth.

3. Remove the chicken from the broth and set aside to cool. Using a soup spoon, scoop out some dumpling dough, round it with another spoon, and drop it into the broth. Repeat this with the rest of the dumpling dough (you should have 10 to 12 balls), cover the pot with a lid, and simmer for 15 to 20 minutes.

4. When the chicken has cooled, shred the meat and discard the bones and skin. Add the meat back into the broth with the cooked dumplings. Ladle the soup into bowls and garnish with the radicchio, cilantro, and lime wedges and serve.

Spicy Parmesan Chicken Potpie

Makes one 9-inch (23cm) pie

Piecrust

2 cups (250g)
all-purpose flour

½ cup plus 1 tablespoon
(125g) unsalted butter, cut
into ½-inch (1.3cm) cubes

1 teaspoon ground
turmeric

½ teaspoon kosher salt

¼ teaspoon coarsely
ground black pepper

1 large egg

6 tablespoons (90ml)
ice-cold water

Filling

One 3- to 4-pound
(1.4 to 1.8kg) chicken cut
in 10 pieces (see page 4),
reserving the backbone
and cutting it into a
few chunks

1 cup (250g) canned
unsalted tomato puree

1 cup (240ml) heavy
cream

1¼ cups (300ml) water

8 garlic cloves, smashed
with the side of a knife as
if you hate them

One 1-inch (2.5cm) piece
of ginger, sliced thickly

1 jalapeño, stemmed,
halved lengthwise,
and unseeded

2 teaspoons garam masala

½ teaspoon pimentón
(smoked Spanish paprika)

¾ teaspoon kosher salt

This chicken potpie has made some excellent life choices. I was going to say this is a chicken potpie "on steroids," but that feels pretty cliché, and this potpie is anything but. When I think of potpie, I think of a salty, creamy stew with chicken, tiny vegetables, and a flaky crust, and this is all of those things—but different. Here, the creaminess comes in the form of a spicy sauce, spiked with saltiness from Parmesan cheese. And let's not forget about our flaky crust, which has turmeric and kind of looks like a giant Jamaican beef patty! You could go out and buy a piecrust and I would never know. Or will I?

1. To make the crust, in a food processor, combine the flour, butter, turmeric, salt, and pepper and pulse a few times. Add the egg and ice-cold water and pulse several more times, until everything looks fairly well incorporated but is still a chunky mess. Dump the dough onto your countertop and push and shove until everything comes together in a ball. You don't want to knead per se, because we don't want to break up the butter too much (butter chunks help create steam, which means flaky crust), but everything should stick together. Put the dough ball in a mixing bowl, cover with plastic wrap, and refrigerate for 30 minutes.

2. To make the filling, while the pie dough is resting, put the chicken parts and bones in a large stockpot. Add the tomato puree, heavy cream, 1 cup (240ml) of the water, the garlic, ginger, jalapeño, garam masala, pimentón, and salt. Bring to a boil, then lower the heat and simmer for 1 hour, stirring occasionally, especially if the chicken bones aren't completely submerged. Pull out the 4 breast pieces after about 30 minutes and reserve.

3. Carefully strain the broth through a medium-mesh sieve into a large measuring cup. You should have about 2 cups (480ml) of liquid. Rinse the pot, return the broth to the pot, and return the pot to the stove. If you have more than 2 cups (480ml) of broth, cook over medium heat until it is reduced to 2 cups (480ml), and if you have less, add enough water to get to 2 cups (480ml). When the strained chicken is cool enough to work with, shred the dark meat, as well as the reserved breast pieces, and put it aside, discarding the bones.

CONTINUED

1½ tablespoons cornstarch

2 ounces (55g) Parmesan, grated

½ cup (70g) English peas (fresh, or frozen and unthawed)

½ cup (60g) pearl onions (fresh, peeled and parboiled, or frozen and unthawed)

1 tablespoon chopped cilantro

4. In a small bowl or cup, combine the cornstarch with the remaining ¼ cup (60ml) water and whisk until dissolved. Pour the slurry into the sauce, bring the sauce to a boil over medium heat while continuously whisking, then turn off the heat. Add the shredded chicken, Parmesan, peas, onions, and cilantro to the thickened sauce and stir to combine. Transfer to a metal bowl and refrigerate to chill completely.

5. Unwrap the chilled pie dough and cut it into two pieces, one a little bit bigger than the other. Take the bigger piece and use a rolling pin to roll it into an approximately 11-inch (28cm) round; you want the dough to be big enough to fill the pie plate with some extra to hang over the edge. Now roll out the smaller ball into a 9½-inch (24cm) round. Layer the dough rounds on a baking sheet, separated by a piece of parchment or wax paper, and refrigerate for 30 minutes.

6. Heat the oven to 400°F (200°C).

7. Butter a 9-inch (23cm) pie plate. Remove the rolled pie dough from the fridge and place the bigger dough round in the pie plate. Return it to the refrigerator until you are ready to assemble the pie—keeping the dough as cold as possible during the assembly will ensure a super flaky crust.

8. Remove the pie plate and the cooled chicken filling from the refrigerator, and pour the chicken mixture into the dough-lined pie plate while listening to Metallica's "For Whom the Bell Tolls" on the album *Ride the Lightning*, because it makes for a great contrast. Then lay the remaining piece of dough over the pie, press it down onto the rim of the pie plate, and, with a sharp knife, trim the excess dough away to the edge of the pie plate. At this point, you can crimp the edges or press the tines of a fork into them, or just leave the sealed edges straight. And you should poke a hole or two in the top crust for steam to escape!

9. Place the pie on a rimmed sheet pan (just in case it bubbles over and makes a mess) and bake for 1 hour, until it is pretty and golden and happy. Remove from the oven and let it rest for 30 minutes before you cut into it. It will be a little loose on the inside, but don't be afraid. You can also let it cool completely and refrigerate it, if you want super-neat slices and like to eat cold food as much as I do.

Chicken & Kimchi Pierogies

Makes 40 dumplings, which serves 8 to 10

Dough

4 cups (500g) all-purpose flour, plus more for dusting

2 egg whites

1 cup (240ml) chicken stock or water, at room temperature

2 tablespoons schmaltz (rendered chicken fat) or neutral oil

½ teaspoon kosher salt

Filling

2 russet potatoes, baked at 400°F (200°C) for 1 hour, or until soft, skin removed

1 cup (240g) prepared kimchi, liquid drained

1 cup (170g) shredded cooked chicken (see page 7)

1½ teaspoons kosher salt

Pinch of red pepper flakes (optional)

Butter, for serving

Apple Salad

1 pound (450g) mixed baby greens

4 crunchy apples (such as Gala or Fuji), cored and very thinly sliced

¼ cup (60g) sour cream

2 teaspoons kosher salt

1 tablespoon freshly squeezed lemon juice

When I was a kid, we used to make the drive every couple of years from Ithaca, New York, to Richmond, Virginia, and along the way we always stopped off the highway at a restaurant called Mom & Pop's Pierogies. From then on, pierogies became something I cared about very deeply. Many years later, when opening my first restaurant, I wanted to serve pierogies but also do something unexpected with them. I thought about traditional fillings, and cabbage leapt out, which made me think of kimchi, one of the great cabbage preparations of the world. So I mixed kimchi with potatoes and put them into pierogies, and everybody rejoiced! Here, I've added cooked chicken to the dumplings to make them heartier. These would be killer with a salad of greens and apples dressed with sour cream and lemon juice, kind of like the applesauce and sour cream you'd traditionally eat with pierogies. They freeze very well, so make a double batch!

1. To make the dough, combine the flour, egg whites, stock, schmaltz, and salt in a mixing bowl and mix thoroughly. Sprinkle a little flour on the counter, turn the dough out onto it, and knead until you feel good about it (it will still look a little rough no matter how well you knead it, but when you press a finger into it, the hole you make should bounce back pretty triumphantly). Wrap the dough ball in plastic wrap and put it in the refrigerator to rest for at least 30 or up to a couple of days.

2. While the dough is resting, see if *Moana* is still on Netflix, in case it also causes your baby daughter to go into an ocean-induced meditative state and allows you to make the filling uninterrupted. To make the filling, mash 2 cups (430g) of the cooked potatoes in a bowl. Place the kimchi and chicken in a food processor and pulse until just chopped and still chunky, then add to the potatoes. Add the salt, mix thoroughly, and taste. If you want to increase the spice level, add the red pepper flakes. Put the filling in the fridge and give your daughter a small cup of blueberries to eat/hide in the couch while you make the dumpling wrappers.

3. Pull the dough out of the fridge, unwrap it, and cut it into eight pieces of equal size. Roll each piece until it's super thin, using flour to keep it from sticking to the counter or the rolling pin. Get the sheets about as thin as you can (about ⅛ inch/3mm thick), as the gluten will cause them to contract a little after being rolled and they will be plenty thick in the end.

CONTINUED

4. With a ring cutter or the widest-diameter drinking glass you own (3 to 4 inches, or 7.5 to 10 cm, in diameter is ideal), cut four rounds out of each sheet. Stack the cut rounds as you work and keep them covered with a towel so they don't dry out. After cutting rounds out of all eight pieces of dough, bunch all of the scraps together, reroll them, and cut out eight more rounds. You should have about forty dumpling wrappers and also a huge sense of accomplishment, because that really was the hard part.

5. Arrange the stack of wrappers on the counter with a little cup of water next to it, along with the bowl of filling and a large plate or baking sheet dusted with flour, leaving yourself space to work in the middle. Put a wrapper on the counter in front of you, dip your index finger into the water cup, and run your finger along the outside edge of the dumpling wrapper to wet it. Put a tablespoon of filling in the middle of the dumpling and fold the edge over. Press the edges of the filled dumpling together, working from the middle outward and keeping close to the filling so that you push any air out. (Hot air trapped inside your dumpling can cause it to burst!) With the tines of a fork, crimp the edge and then put the pierogi on your floured plate. Repeat to make the remaining dumplings.

6. If you do not plan on cooking the pierogies right away, arrange them in a single layer on a sheet pan (or two), place in the freezer, and freeze completely before storing in a ziplock freezer bag. These will last for several months.

7. Bring a large pot of water to a boil and cook the pierogies in the boiling water until they float, about 6 minutes (8 minutes if pierogies have been frozen). Drain them and toss with a little butter while they are still hot.

8. To make the apple salad, in a mixing bowl, combine the greens, apples, sour cream, salt, and lemon juice. Toss well.

9. Serve the pierogies with the dressed apple salad on the side.

Szechuan Pepper–Lacquered Chicken

Serves 4

1 cup (230g) kosher salt

4 limes, halved

¼ cup (50g) Szechuan
peppercorns

2 heads garlic, split

6 tablespoons (90ml)
maple syrup

2 tablespoons soy sauce

1 teaspoon red
pepper flakes

1 teaspoon ground sage

10 cups (2.4L) cold water

2 cups (240g) ice

One 3- to 4-pound
(1.4 to 1.8kg) chicken

Cucumber Salad

1 large cucumber
(standard or hothouse),
or 4 to 5 Persian
cucumbers, sliced into
¼-inch (6mm) rounds

¼ red onion, thinly sliced

1 garlic clove,
finely minced

2 teaspoons kosher salt

2 teaspoons distilled
white vinegar

1 teaspoon extra-virgin
olive oil

Do you ever feel like roasting a chicken is too easy (see page 3 for evidence)? Like maybe life would be better if there were a more complicated way? Well, I am here for you. I have been obsessed with the roast chickens from a store around the corner, called R&D Foods. Their perfectly juicy roast chickens have the glossiest, most beautifully lacquered skin. But the skin isn't sticky like it was brushed with soy sauce and honey—it's a drier, more seasoned effect. I finally asked the owner, Ilene, how she does it, and it turns out she doesn't baste or glaze the chicken but instead *brines* it with honey to make the skin caramelize super effectively. My recipe starts with Ilene's brine and adds all sorts of things to make it extremely overcomplicated! Just kidding. This chicken is not difficult, but it requires 24 hours to brine. And thanks to all that water, the impact of the brine is relatively mild and the ingredients come together in a mellow way. So this chicken would be equally as comfortable with mashed potatoes and gravy (see page 98) as with a big cucumber salad.

1. In a stockpot, combine the salt, limes, peppercorns, garlic, maple syrup, soy sauce, red pepper flakes, sage, and 4 cups (950ml) of the water. Turn the heat to high, bring the water to a boil, turn off the heat, and add the ice and remaining 6 cups (1.4L) water. Stir until the ice is melted. The brine absorbs tons of flavor when it's heated, but we want it to cool completely before introducing the chicken, for food safety reasons.

2. Transfer the brine to a large container and add the chicken. Cover and refrigerate; don't even look at it for at least 24 hours or up to 48 hours.

3. Heat the oven to 450°F (230°C). Remove the chicken from the brine and pat it dry. Put it on a cooling rack above a sheet pan and let it air dry while the oven heats. Roast for about 1 hour, rotating the pan halfway through, until the skin is super dark and beautiful and the internal temperature is about 165°F (75°C). I won't bother talking about the color of the juices here—for my feelings about that, read the note on page 8.

4. To make the cucumber salad, while the chicken is roasting, combine the cucumber, onion, garlic, salt, vinegar, and oil in a bowl and mix well.

5. Remove the chicken from the oven and let it rest for 10 minutes before carving. Serve with the cucumber salad.

Chicken Choucroute Garnie

Serves 4 to 6

Brine

2 cups (480ml) water

¼ cup (70g) kosher salt

1 tablespoon honey

3 garlic cloves, smashed

2 teaspoons whole black peppercorns

¼ teaspoon ground allspice

8 bags lapsang souchong tea

2 cups (240g) ice

1½ pounds (680g) bone-in, skin-on chicken breasts or thighs

2 pounds (900g) ground chicken, or 2½ pounds (1.1kg) boneless, skinless chicken thighs, for grinding

Sausage #1

2 teaspoons finely minced garlic

1 teaspoon kosher salt

½ teaspoon garam masala

¼ teaspoon red pepper flakes

¼ teaspoon smoked paprika

My first professional cooking job after graduating from culinary school was actually in the restaurant at the culinary school itself because I am lazy. I was surrounded by professional chefs who were all happy to share their knowledge, among them André Soltner. He is an amazingly talented Alsatian chef who taught me how to make head cheese (it is safe to say I will never forget Chef Soltner). When I was asked to come up with a menu for a private dinner for about twenty people at the school's restaurant, I chose to make choucroute garnie—a French dish by way of Germany, usually made by braising various pork products in sauerkraut—in Chef Soltner's honor. With chicken, the choucroute is so much lighter and brighter than using a bunch of pork sausages and hams that I may only make it this way from now on. The chicken sausages in this recipe are spiced in contrasting ways—one with garam masala and garlic, the other with fennel and coriander—since a traditional choucroute's sausages would be made pretty differently to pair nicely with one another (Jacques Pépin's recipe, for example, calls for kielbasa and hot dogs). We'll cook all of it in beer, which is nontraditional, but I was born in Wisconsin and I want there to be beer in that pot.

1. To make the brine, combine the water, salt, honey, garlic, peppercorns, and allspice in a small saucepan and bring to a boil over high heat. Turn the heat to low and simmer for 5 minutes. Turn off the heat, add the tea bags, and let stand for another 5 minutes. Transfer the brine to a large container, add the ice and the bone-in, skin-on chicken, and stir everything to combine. Cover the container and refrigerate for 24 hours.

2. If you're grinding the chicken yourself, cut the boneless, skinless chicken thighs for the two sausages into even 1-inch (2.5cm) pieces. Working in small batches, place the chicken in your food processor and pulse to finely chop, but avoid turning it into a mousse.

3. To make sausage #1, add half of the ground chicken to a mixing bowl. Combine the chicken in the bowl with the garlic, salt, garam masala, red pepper flakes, and smoked paprika and mix very well.

CONTINUED

Sausage #2

1 teaspoon kosher salt

1 teaspoon freshly ground black pepper

½ teaspoon ground coriander

½ teaspoon dried thyme

½ teaspoon fennel seeds

¼ teaspoon dried oregano

To Assemble

1 tablespoon vegetable oil, plus more as needed

4 garlic cloves, smashed

½ large yellow onion, thinly sliced

2 cups (480ml) chicken stock

1 cup (240ml) non-hoppy beer

2 pounds (900g) sauerkraut, rinsed, drained, and squeezed

1 pound (450g) baby red potatoes

8 dried juniper berries, crushed

2 bay leaves

½ teaspoon caraway seed

¼ cup (5g) parsley leaves, for garnish

Whichever mustard you like the best, for serving

4. To make sausage #2, place the remaining ground chicken in another mixing bowl. Add the salt, pepper, coriander, thyme, fennel seeds, and oregano and mix very well.

5. Form the meat into balls about 2 inches (5cm) in diameter. Refrigerate the sausage until you are ready to make the choucroute.

6. When you are ready to assemble the choucroute, heat the oven to 400°F (200°C). Remove the chicken from the brine and pat it dry. In a large ovenproof sauté pan or Dutch oven, heat the oil over high heat until it starts to smoke. Sear the chicken until lightly browned, 5 to 7 minutes on each side. Remove the chicken from the pan and set aside on a plate. Adding another teaspoon or two of oil if necessary, place both types of sausage into the pot, flipping the sausage until lightly browned on all sides, 7 to 10 minutes. Remove the sausage and set aside. Add the garlic and cook until fragrant, about 5 minutes. Add the onion and cook, stirring, until it is lightly caramelized, about 5 minutes more. Add the stock, beer, sauerkraut, potatoes, juniper berries, bay leaves, and caraway seeds; bring to a boil; then turn the heat to medium. Simmer, stirring occasionally, until the liquid has reduced by half and the potatoes are tender, about 20 minutes.

7. Nestle the seared chicken and sausage into the sauerkraut. Put the whole thing in the oven for 20 to 25 minutes, or until the chicken and sausage are no longer pink, the sauerkraut is starting to brown a little, and your whole apartment smells so good that you can't wait any longer.

8. Remove the pot from the oven and scoop everything out onto a platter, leaving behind the bay leaves and any excess broth. Garnish with the parsley and serve with plenty of mustard on the side!

Chicken & Shrimp Dumplings

Makes 48 dumplings, which serves 8

Pickled Red Onions

1 small red onion, sliced into thin rounds

1 cup (240ml) distilled white vinegar

½ teaspoon kosher salt

Dumpling Wrappers

4 cups (500g) all-purpose flour, plus more as needed

2 packets (about 2 teaspoons) Sazón Goya

1½ cups (355ml) water

2 egg whites

Filling

One 1-inch (2.5cm) piece ginger, peeled and sliced thinly against the grain

1 bunch scallions, white and green parts, roughly chopped

4 chipotles in adobo sauce

1 pound (450g) shrimp, peeled and deveined

1 pound (450g) ground chicken, or 1¼ pounds (570g) boneless, skinless chicken thighs, for grinding

2 teaspoons dry vermouth

2 teaspoons distilled white vinegar

1 teaspoon kosher salt

½ teaspoon toasted sesame oil

¼ teaspoon ground cumin

These dumplings are inspired in part by the pork and shrimp shu mai of Hong Kong, combined with a little heat from smoked jalapeños from Mexico, and cumin, sesame seeds, and cilantro, ingredients that I can't pin down to a particular region because most of the world has agreed they are delicious. I dress the dumplings with pickled red onions, olive oil, and chunks of avocado, so we don't need a dipping sauce (the onions have plenty of acid and flavor) and we still get a good amount of heft in each bite (thank you, avocados). And I like how cilantro and sesame seeds are just as much Central American as they are Chinese, and how that ambiguity suits these ambiguous dumplings nicely! You certainly don't have to make your own dumpling wrappers—there are lots of good ones available online or at the grocery store, like the Gyoza No Kawa or Dynasty brands—but if you don't make your own, you won't be able to put Sazón Goya (a Latin American seasoning blend containing coriander, garlic, cumin, and achiote, which makes it bright orange and super fun) into the dough. By the way, my recipe for dumpling wrappers is basically straight from Helen You's *Dumpling Galaxy Cookbook*, but I swapped the salt for the Sazón Goya I mentioned.

1. To pickle the red onion, combine the onion, vinegar, and salt in a small mixing bowl, mix well, and pour into a nonreactive container with a lid. Let the mixture marinate in the refrigerator for at least 1 hour or up to the next Ice Age (which might not be that long from now, so try to eat your pickled onions within 2 weeks!).

2. To make the wrappers, combine the flour and Sazón Goya in a mixing bowl and stir together. Add the water and egg whites and mix thoroughly, adding a touch of flour to your hands and kneading until the dough is relatively smooth and springy, 2 to 3 minutes. Wrap the dough in plastic wrap and let it rest in the fridge for 30 minutes.

3. While the dough rests, make the filling. In a food processor, combine the ginger, scallions, and chipotles with 4 teaspoons of their sauce. Pulse until well chopped, scraping down the processor's sides a couple of times to make sure everything is incorporated. Add the shrimp and pulse some more until it comes together but is not quite a paste. Put the shrimp filling in a mixing bowl. If you're grinding the chicken yourself, first cut the meat into even

CONTINUED

To Serve

4 ripe avocados, peeled, pitted, and cubed

1 cup (40g) cilantro leaves, chopped

Extra-virgin olive oil, for drizzling

2 tablespoons black sesame seeds (optional, but they look so cool!)

1-inch (2.5cm) pieces. Working in small batches, place the chicken in your food processor and pulse to finely chop, but avoid turning it into a mousse. Add the ground chicken to the mixing bowl with the shrimp, along with the vermouth, vinegar, salt, sesame oil, and cumin, mixing all of it thoroughly with your hands. Put the filling in the fridge.

4. Now, let's roll out the dumpling wrappers! Pull out the dough from the refrigerator and turn it out onto the lightly floured counter. Roll it into a log shape and cut the log into 16 pieces of equal size. Now cut each of those 16 pieces in thirds to get 48 even-ish pieces. We did it! With some more flour and your amazingly useful and deft hands, roll each piece into a beautiful little ball that looks good enough to eat (but please do not eat the raw dough). Dust the balls with flour, one at a time, and roll them out to 2½ to 3 inches (6.5 to 7.5cm) in diameter. If you flour your wrappers well before rolling them out, you should be able to just stack them up. Keep the stacked wrappers covered with a dish towel to prevent them from drying out.

5. Make yourself a little dumpling-assembly station, with a cup of water for wetting the wrappers, a floured sheet pan for the filled dumplings to land on, and a couple of spoons for scooping filling. Oh, and pull the filling out of the fridge! One at a time, wet the circumference of a dumpling wrapper with your gorgeous finger and then scoop about ½ tablespoon of filling right into the middle. Fold one end of the wrapper over to the other to create a half moon. Pick up the dumpling and press the air out of either end with your fingers while sealing it up—you can crimp it if you like. Put the dumpling onto the floured sheet pan and repeat with the rest of the wrappers.

6. If you're not eating all the dumplings now, arrange them in a single layer on a lined sheet pan, put them in the freezer so they freeze completely, and, once frozen, store them in a ziplock freezer bag for several months. Bring a large pot of water to a boil, add the dumplings, and cook, stirring occasionally, until they float to the top and feel firm to the touch, 4 to 6 minutes (6 to 8 minutes if cooking from frozen). The dumplings can now be plated as is, or you can pat them dry and crisp them up in an oiled nonstick pan over medium-high heat.

7. To serve, put six dumplings on each plate with half a cubed avocado. Top with some of the pickled red onions, a bunch of chopped cilantro, a drizzle of olive oil, and a sprinkling of black sesame seeds (if using).

Chicken Confit with Pickled Tomatoes

Serves 8

8 bone-in, skin-on chicken thighs, 3 to 4 pounds (1.4 to 1.8kg)

¼ cup (55g) kosher salt

4 teaspoons ras el hanout

1 head garlic, cloves peeled and smashed

24 sprigs fresh thyme

Pickled Tomatoes

¾ cup (175ml) distilled white vinegar

½ cup (120ml) water

1½ tablespoons molasses

2 teaspoons kosher salt

1 teaspoon vanilla extract

1 pint (285g) grape tomatoes, quartered

½ yellow onion, diced

12 sprigs fresh thyme

1 yellow onion, thinly sliced

1½ cups (355ml) extra-virgin olive oil

1½ cups (355ml) vegetable oil

Herby Rice Noodle Salad

2 pounds (900g) cooked rice vermicelli

2 cups (80g) chopped herbs (such as parsley, mint, basil, or dill)

2 teaspoons kosher salt

Confit is one of those old-fashioned food preservation things that we still do because it's delicious. After meat is salted and braised in its own fat, it can safely sit, submerged in that fat, for weeks, without spoiling. Until the zombie apocalypse, we have refrigeration, but that doesn't mean we can't also have confit. This confited chicken is spiced with ras el hanout, a North African spice mix (I like the one from New York Shuk), which will make you feel warm inside and confidently charming on the outside. My favorite way to serve this confit is to crisp it up and pile it on top of herby, confit fat–dressed rice noodles. I garnish with bright pickled tomatoes, slightly sweetened with earthy molasses and floral vanilla to cut through it all.

1. Put the chicken, salt, ras el hanout, garlic, and thyme in a ziplock freezer bag. Seal the bag and shake vigorously. Put the bag in a plastic container to prevent leakage, and refrigerate for 12 to 24 hours.

2. To pickle the tomatoes, combine the vinegar, water, molasses, salt, and vanilla in a nonreactive container with a tight-fitting lid. Cover and shake to completely dissolve the salt. Add the tomatoes, onion, and thyme and mix well. Cover and refrigerate for at least 1 hour or up to 2 weeks.

3. Heat the oven to 225°F (110°C). Remove the bag with the chicken from the refrigerator. Pour the contents into a colander in the sink and rinse. Transfer the chicken, garlic, and thyme sprigs to an 8 by 8-inch (20 by 20cm) baking dish with fairly high sides, or a Dutch oven, so that the chicken sits in one layer. Spread the sliced onion on top and pour in the oils, until the chicken is completely covered. Bake for 6 hours, or until the onion has caramelized and the chicken is super tender and delicious and falling off of the bone. Carefully pull the dish out of the oven to cool for an hour, then remove the chicken and strain the fat into a clean lidded jar (it'll keep in the fridge for months). Shred the cooked chicken and set aside on a large plate.

4. To make the noodle salad, in a bowl, toss the rice noodles with the herbs, ½ cup of the reserved confit fat, and the salt.

5. Heat 2 teaspoons of the confit fat in a large nonstick pan over high heat until it just starts to smoke. Add the shredded chicken confit and cook for 10 minutes, stirring occasionally, until the meat is browned, crispy, and insanely fragrant. Divide the noodle salad among eight bowls, top with the sautéed confit and some pickled tomatoes, and serve.

Party Chicken to
Impress Guests
(& Celebrities!)

Grilled Chicken Tacos, Three Ways

Serves 4

1 to 1½ pounds (450 to 680g) boneless, skinless chicken breasts or thighs

¼ onion, thinly sliced

¼ cup (60ml) orange juice

1 tablespoon tahini

2 teaspoons kosher salt

1 teaspoon ancho chile powder

1 teaspoon cumin seeds

1 lime, halved

1 tablespoon extra-virgin olive oil

Corn or flour tortillas, for serving

Earlier, I went on about how hard I strived not to write recipes for you that involved watered-down versions of amazing dishes from other countries, and here we are with chicken tacos, and you're confused. And so am I! But since I consider every food to be either a sandwich or a future sandwich, I'm using the word *taco* pretty loosely to describe chicken that is folded in flatbread (specifically, tortillas). The marinade here draws inspiration from several marinades spanning the globe, and the suggested toppings follow suit. Choose one or all of them, and no one will be sad.

1. In a ziplock freezer bag, combine the chicken, onion, orange juice, tahini, salt, chile powder, and cumin seeds. Squeeze the lime juice into the bag and throw in the rinds as well. Seal the bag and shake well. Put the bag in a bowl or plastic container to prevent leakage, and refrigerate overnight or for up to 24 hours.

2. Heat a grill to the Gold Particles Smashing in a Super Collider setting, or the highest it can go.

3. Remove the chicken from the marinade, shaking off any excess, and transfer it to a large mixing bowl. Add the oil and toss to completely coat. Grill the chicken, turning occasionally, until it is nicely charred, about 10 minutes. Pull it from the grill and let it rest for a couple minutes before slicing into ½-inch-thick (1.3cm-thick) strips.

4. Heat the tortillas on the grill for 30 seconds, flipping once, or until they are warmed through. Top with the chicken and any of the following extras on the opposite page before serving.

Taco Extras for Extra-Special Friends & Family

While I see absolutely nothing wrong with eating just marinated grilled chicken piled into a freshly grilled tortilla any night of the week, here are some extras to make that already winning combination almost unfairly good.

Salsa Más Macha (page 65) + Salted Cucumbers

To the warmed tortillas with the chicken, toss in a few ¼-inch-thick (6mm-thick) slices of unpeeled, unseeded cucumbers seasoned with a pinch of kosher salt, and scoop on a heaping teaspoon of salsa más macha.

Grilled Eggplant + Yogurt

Cut one eggplant into ½-inch-thick (1.3cm-thick) round slices. Toss them in a mixture of 2 teaspoons freshly squeezed lime juice, 1 teaspoon kosher salt, and 1 teaspoon extra-virgin olive oil. Grill, turning occasionally, for about 10 minutes. Add a few slices to your taco with a dollop of full-fat plain yogurt.

Quick-Pickled Vegetables + Sliced Avocado

Any kind of pickled vegetable is awesome on tacos! I like beets, cauliflower, and cucumber. To make the pickles, in a mixing bowl, combine 1 cup (340g) bite-size veggies with ½ cup (120ml) distilled white vinegar, 1 tablespoon salt, and 1 tablespoon granulated sugar. Mix well, transfer to a lidded nonreactive container, and cover and refrigerate for 1 hour (or up to 2 weeks). Peel, pit, and slice 2 avocados. To the warmed tacos, add a palmful of drained pickled vegetables and a few slices of avocado.

Chickensagna

Serves 6 to 8

Tomato Sauce

2 tablespoons extra-virgin olive oil

8 garlic cloves, smashed

¼ cup (60ml) heavy cream

1 teaspoon kosher salt

One 28-ounce (794g) can crushed tomatoes

Sautéed Fennel

2 fennel bulbs, cut root to tip into ¼-inch (6mm) slices

1 tablespoon extra-virgin olive oil

2 teaspoons fennel seeds

¼ teaspoon kosher salt

¼ cup (60ml) freshly squeezed lemon juice

Ground Chicken Filling

8 ounces (225g) ground chicken, or 12 ounces (340g) boneless, skinless chicken thighs, for grinding

1 tablespoon extra-virgin olive oil

1 small yellow onion, thinly sliced

1 small green bell pepper, stem and seeds removed, thinly sliced

1 teaspoon kosher salt

¼ teaspoon dried thyme

¼ teaspoon dried oregano

What if I told you that I invented a lasagna-like casserole made entirely of chicken that contained zero pasta? I can hear you asking it now: "Why would you want to do that?" I'm not really sure either, because I think chicken and pasta are perfectly amazing together (see pages 19 and 146). But neither lasagna, nor ricotta cheese, are things I ate often growing up or have ever been super excited about. That all changed when I met my wife, Katherine, as her love of lasagna soon became our shared love of lasagna. And I have a hard time eating any pasta without ricotta since we fell in love (I mean, my wife and I, even though ricotta and I have become quite close). So I started obsessing over lasagna and its ricotta filling, inventing all kinds of crazy permutations—from chicken jus-sauced noodles with ricotta to a huge ricotta-stuffed red snapper, braised in a fennel-infused tomato sauce. And I ultimately arrived somewhere in the middle, at this chickensagna: Pounded boneless, skinless chicken (breasts, thighs, or both) are dredged with flour and piled into a casserole, between layers of tomato sauce, lemony fennel, and a creamy ricotta filling. To me, it makes perfect sense.

All of the work and finesse in this chickensagna happen during assembly, so it's great for entertaining; you can simply cook and serve it without any last-minute fussing, and enjoy a glass of wine or a boilermaker with casual grace as your guests arrive. It can also be assembled ahead of time and kept in the fridge before baking—just give yourself an hour to cook it and an extra 30 minutes to let it rest before serving. Serve it with a loaf of crusty bread and a salad if you really want to go for it.

1. To make the sauce, heat the oil in a saucepan over medium heat. Add the garlic and cook for 5 to 6 minutes, until lightly browned. Add the heavy cream and salt and stir to combine. Stir in the crushed tomatoes, bring to a boil, turn the heat to low, and simmer for 20 minutes, or until thick and awesome.

2. Meanwhile, to make the fennel, in a separate sauté pan, combine the sliced fennel, oil, fennel seeds, and salt and sauté over medium heat until lightly caramelized. Add the lemon juice and cook, stirring regularly, until the liquid

CONTINUED

Ricotta Filling

15 ounces (425g) whole-milk ricotta

1 cup (110g) shredded part-skim, low-moisture mozzarella

½ cup (50g) grated Parmesan

½ teaspoon kosher salt

1 egg

1 cup (20g) torn or roughly chopped basil leaves

Chicken "Noodles"

3 pounds (1.4kg) boneless, skinless chicken (breasts, thighs, or both)

5 tablespoons (40g) all-purpose flour

½ teaspoon kosher salt

To Assemble

1½ cups (170g) shredded part-skim, low-moisture mozzarella

Loaf of crusty bread, for serving

has completely evaporated and the fennel is tender, 8 to 10 minutes. If it is not yet tender, add a splash of water and continue cooking a little longer. Transfer the fennel to a bowl and wipe out the pan.

3. Next, make the ground chicken filling. If you're grinding the chicken yourself, cut the meat into even 1-inch (2.5cm) pieces. Working in small batches, place the chicken in your food processor and pulse to finely chop, but avoid turning it into a mousse. To cook the ground chicken, add the oil to the pan you used to cook the fennel and heat over high heat. When the oil starts to smoke, add all of the ground chicken and cook until it begins to brown, 7 to 10 minutes. Add the onion, bell pepper, salt, thyme, and oregano and stir, breaking up the chicken into small pieces. Cook until the onion and bell pepper are tender but still crunchy, about 10 minutes.

4. To make the ricotta filling, combine the ricotta, mozzarella, Parmesan, salt, egg, and basil in a mixing bowl and mix thoroughly.

5. To prepare the chicken "noodles," with a very sharp knife and steady hands, slice the chicken lengthwise into the thinnest pieces you can, approximately ¼ inch (6mm) thick. I can get four slices out of a breast and three out of a thigh. Using a big piece of plastic wrap (like you did to pound the chicken on page 16!) and a meat hammer or the flat bottom of a pan, beat all of your cares out of the slices so that they are even thinner—about ⅛ inch (3mm) in thickness—and approximately three times the size. Put your pounded slices in a mixing bowl, add the flour and salt, and toss, coating every slice of chicken well.

6. Let's put everything together because we've made it this far and may as well keep going. Right? Right! First, heat the oven to 350°F (175°C).

7. Spoon a little of the tomato sauce in the bottom of a 9 by 13-inch (23 by 33cm) baking dish. Lay one-third of the pounded chicken slices in a layer over the sauce, letting them overlap slightly (they will shrink as they cook). Spread half of the ricotta filling across the chicken. Top the ricotta with half of the ground chicken filling, half of the sautéed fennel, and more sauce. Repeat that whole process, and finally top it with the remaining chicken slices, sauce, and the mozzarella. You did it!

8. Bake the casserole for 1 hour, or until the cheese is brown and bubbly. If you want it a little bit darker on the top, broil it for a couple minutes at the end. Remove the chickensagna from the oven and let rest for 30 to 60 minutes before serving with crusty bread.

Chicken Pot-au-Feu

Serves 6 to 8

One 3- to 4-pound
(1.4 to 1.8kg) chicken

2 tablespoons kosher salt

12 sprigs fresh thyme

1 shallot, thinly sliced

2 teaspoons freshly
ground black pepper

**Scallion-Horseradish
Sauce**

One 2-inch (5cm)
piece fresh horseradish,
sliced into ¼-inch
(6mm) rounds

1 bunch scallions,
white and green parts,
roughly cut into ¼-inch
(6mm) slices

2 teaspoons kosher salt

1 cup (240ml) peanut oil

**Sweet Mustard
Crème Fraîche**

½ cup (115g)
crème fraîche

¼ cup (60g) sweet
chili sauce

¼ bunch dill,
finely chopped

2 tablespoons
whole-grain mustard

½ teaspoon kosher salt

Pot-au-feu is the absolute funnest way to serve boiled food (not necessarily always the funnest food). It is traditionally made by boiling tough cuts of beef, maybe some marrow bones, and a bunch of vegetables all together in water, and then serving the resulting broth as an appetizer followed by a second course of the meat and vegetables with exciting sauces for dipping. For this chicken pot-au-feu, I use the Chinese "white-cut" method, a traditional poaching technique that involves simmering the chicken in water for a relatively short period of time and then turning off the heat, covering the pot, and letting the chicken sit and poach and get all silky and juicy. After pulling the chicken meat off its bones, put the bones back in the broth to mingle with the vegetables, which can be whatever you like, really. We'll serve it with some crusty bread, a creamy mustard sauce with the surprise additions of Thai sweet chili and dill, and a Chinese scallion-horseradish sauce that I stole from my friend Francis Lam and then tweaked a little. This fairly hands-off project does take a couple of days, but it makes for a totally manageable, still super-impressive party.

1. Place the chicken in a ziplock freezer bag and season it inside and out with the salt. Add the thyme, shallot, and pepper; seal the bag; and give it a good shake to make sure that everything is more or less distributed. Put the bag in a bowl or plastic container to prevent leakage, and refrigerate overnight or for up to 24 hours.

2. While the chicken brines, make the scallion-horseradish sauce. Put the horseradish in a food processor and pulse until well chopped. Add the scallions and pulse until everything is about the same size. Transfer the mixture to a metal mixing bowl with sides that are high enough to hold 3 cups of liquid (we're using only a cup, but it can bubble way up and we want to be safe!). Add the salt and stir to mix. In a small saucepan, heat the peanut oil until it begins to smoke. Pour it over the scallion and horseradish mixture, stir, and let the mixture cool to room temperature. Refrigerate in a plastic container with a lid for several weeks or until you eat all of it on everything. Give the sauce a stir before serving.

CONTINUED

12 cups (2.8L) water

1 tablespoon honey

1 tablespoon low-sodium soy sauce

1 pound (450g) baby turnips, greens removed and washed but kept separate

1 bunch scallions, white and green parts, roots removed

2 large carrots, peeled and quartered

1 pound (450g) asparagus, tough ends removed

Loaf of crusty bread, for serving

3. To make the sweet mustard crème fraîche, in a small mixing bowl, combine the crème fraîche, chili sauce, dill, mustard, and salt and stir well. Refrigerate in a small container with a lid for up to 1 week.

4. After the chicken has brined, remove it from the bag, give it a quick rinse, and discard the thyme and shallot. Put the chicken in your largest stockpot and add the water. Bring the water to a simmer over high heat, turn the heat to low, and simmer the chicken for 30 minutes. Turn off the heat, cover the pot, and let the chicken sit for another 30 minutes. Using a pair of tongs, with one side inserted into the chicken's neck cavity and the other side on its back, pull the chicken out of the pot, let it drain, and transfer to a plate to rest.

5. Season the broth left over in the pot with the honey and soy sauce. Bring it up to a boil, turn the heat to a simmer, taste for seasoning, and adjust if necessary.

6. When the chicken is cool enough to handle, carve it into 10 pieces as you would break down a chicken (see pages 4 to 5), keeping the breasts, thighs, and drumsticks whole and doing your best to keep the skin intact. Carefully remove the bones from the breasts and thighs and reserve. Slice each piece of chicken crosswise into ½-inch (1.3cm) slices (leave the drumsticks and wings whole and bone-in) and arrange them on a platter large enough to accommodate the chicken and all of the veggies. Cover the chicken with a piece of foil to keep it warm.

7. Put the reserved chicken bones into the broth and add the turnips, scallions, and carrots. Simmer for 30 minutes, or until the vegetables are very tender. Add the asparagus and turnip greens in tight bunches, cooking for 5 to 10 minutes, or until they're pretty tender but still a bit green.

8. Remove the foil from the chicken and ladle a bit of hot broth onto it on the platter. Arrange the vegetables on the platter around the chicken, keeping each type of vegetable together with its friends so that they look cool.

9. Serve everybody some broth in little bowls. While they're eating it, bring out the platter of chicken and vegetables, the sauces to dip everything into, and some crusty bread.

Cornell Chicken

Serves 4 to 8, depending on how much chicken your friends can eat

½ cup (120ml) white
wine vinegar

¼ cup (60ml) vegetable oil

2 eggs

1 tablespoon kosher salt

1 tablespoon ground sage

2 teaspoons ground thyme

2 teaspoons finely ground
black pepper

2 teaspoons cracked
black pepper

1½ teaspoons ground
marjoram

1 teaspoon ground
rosemary

1 teaspoon dried oregano

¾ teaspoon ground
nutmeg

Two 3- to 4-pound
(1.4 to 1.8kg) chickens

If you've never spent a summer in central New York, then you've likely never had one of the greatest additions to the culinary world, Cornell Chicken, for which we have Robert Baker to thank. (You can read about Professor Baker's many feats of culinary genius in the introduction to this book.) It's simple: Halved chickens are marinated in a creamy, tart vinaigrette, and cooked over charcoal by somebody's parents at an outdoor barbecue by the lake or by a volunteer fire department at a roadside fundraising event. The dish is often served with salt potatoes (another upstate favorite involving boiled baby potatoes with a delicious, salty crust) and soda from my favorite grocery store, Wegmans. The marinade is somewhere in between a Carolina-style, vinegar-based barbecue sauce and a creamy Italian dressing from the grocery store, so it's a little tangy, nice and smoky, and entirely unconcerned about your definition of barbecue. Cornell chicken gets even better when you make it at home because you can char it to your heart's desire, and the marinade stays adhered to the chicken thanks to the eggs. At my restaurant, we serve half a chicken as a portion for one, but two chickens could totally feed up to eight people, especially with a bunch of fun sides, like salt potatoes and three-bean salad.

1. In a blender, combine the vinegar, oil, eggs, salt, herbs, and spices and puree until smooth.

2. Cut out the spines of the chickens as if you were spatchcocking them (see page 6), but then instead of removing the breastbone, simply cut directly through it, splitting the chickens in half lengthwise. Put the chickens in a couple of ziplock freezer bags and pour the marinade over them. Put the bags in a large plastic container to prevent leakage and refrigerate for 12 to 24 hours.

3. Heat the grill to the black leather interior of a parked car on a 100°F (38°C) day, or as hot as it will go. Pull the chicken from the marinade and put it on the grill, skin-side down. Grill, turning occasionally, until the chicken is cooked through, about 30 minutes—it should get to an internal temperature of about 165°F/75°C. Remember that if the skin side is getting too dark, you can cook the chicken longer on the bone side!

4. Cut the halved chickens into pieces (like how we'd break down a chicken—see page 4) and serve, or just put them on a platter whole next to a bucket of beers (preferably from Ithaca Beer Company)!

Citrus Roast Chicken with Pan Gravy & Sides

Serves 4

One 3- to 4-pound (1.4 to 1.8kg) chicken

2 pounds (900g) assorted citrus

1 tablespoon plus 1 teaspoon extra-virgin olive oil

1 tablespoon kosher salt

½ small shallot, thinly sliced

¼ teaspoon dried rosemary

¼ teaspoon ancho chile powder

½ bunch fresh thyme

Green Bean Salad

2 teaspoons kosher salt

1 pound (450g) green beans or haricots verts, trimmed

3 tablespoons full-fat plain yogurt

½ small shallot, thinly sliced

2 teaspoons freshly squeezed lemon juice

2 teaspoons maple syrup

1 garlic clove, minced

Sometimes I wish I could eat a roast bird and mashed potatoes and gravy for every meal. Most times, I just want somebody to pour gravy all over everything I eat. This chicken-stock gravy is pretty straightforward (just the pan drippings deglazed with chicken stock and thickened with cornstarch), but it's spiked with a little soy sauce for extra umami and Dijon mustard to give it a little kick. And, oh yeah, alongside the gravy, there's, like, a juicy roast chicken with an amazing bounty of citrus. There's also a nontraditional but super delicious mashed sweet- and russet-potato dish with a ribbon of toasted nuts and seeds and fried shallots running through it. And there's also a righteous green bean salad with a lemony yogurt sauce. And all of these are full of things that make you feel alive. Like gravy!

You can just season this chicken and put it in the oven (I don't waste time trussing, see page 8 for why), and make the sides while it cooks. About an hour later you have a magnificent roast chicken dinner. And you also have bones to make stock (see page 9) to use for gravy the next time you roast a chicken!

1. Heat the oven to 400°F (200°C). Put the chicken in a roasting pan. Zest the citrus in a small mixing bowl, add the oil, salt, shallot, rosemary, and chile powder and stir together. Rub the zesty spiced oil all over the whole chicken. Cut the zested fruit into wedges, toss it with the thyme, and stuff it in the cavity of the chicken. Roast the chicken for 1 hour and 15 minutes (the internal temperature should be about 165°F/75°C). If the skin isn't dark enough for your liking, turn on the broiler and get it a little darker.

2. While the chicken is cooking, make the green bean salad. Fill a pot with water, add 1 teaspoon of the salt, and bring to a boil over high heat. Add the green beans to the boiling water and cook until they are the way you like them. I prefer mine to be pretty well cooked, which takes 6 to 8 minutes; for crunchier beans, cook for 4 to 5 minutes. While the beans are cooking, in a large bowl, mix together the yogurt, shallot, lemon juice, maple syrup, garlic, and remaining 1 teaspoon salt. Drain the beans and immediately toss them with the dressing. This salad is great at room temperature or even cold, so don't worry about trying to keep it warm.

CONTINUED

Mashed Potatoes

2 russet potatoes, peeled and cut into 1-inch (2.5cm) cubes

1 large sweet potato, peeled and quartered

½ cup (60g) mixed nuts

2 tablespoons raw, unsalted sunflower seeds

2 tablespoons poppy seeds

2 tablespoons sesame seeds

1 tablespoon fried shallots (store-bought is great)

1 teaspoon kosher salt

1 tablespoon unsalted butter

⅓ cup (80ml) whole milk

Gravy

2 cups (480ml) chicken stock

1 shallot, cut in half

1 teaspoon low-sodium soy sauce

1 teaspoon Dijon mustard

½ teaspoon kosher salt

1 tablespoon cornstarch

3. To make the mashed potatoes, put the russet potatoes and sweet potato in a pot and add water to just barely cover them. Over high heat, bring the water up to a boil, turn the heat to low, and simmer until both the russet potatoes and sweet potato are tender, about 10 minutes. While the potatoes are cooking, put the nuts, sunflower seeds, poppy seeds, and sesame seeds in a dry sauté pan and toast over medium heat until fragrant, about 5 minutes. Put the nut and seed mixture into a food processor, add the fried shallots and salt, and process until well chopped and pastelike. When the potatoes are cooked, drain them and put in a mixing bowl. Add the nut paste, butter, and milk and mash with a potato masher until everything looks integrated and happy—chunky or smooth to your preference.

4. When the chicken is cooked, take it out of the oven and transfer it to a tray or chopping board to rest.

5. To make the gravy, put the roasting pan on the stove and, without removing any of the liquid from the pan, pour in 1 cup (240ml) of the stock, turn the heat to medium-high, and scrape the bottom of the pan to loosen any crispy, caramelized bits. Pour the contents of the roasting pan into a small saucepan and add the shallot, soy sauce, mustard, and salt. In a small bowl, whisk the cornstarch into the remaining 1 cup (240ml) stock and then add the slurry to the pot. Increase the heat to high and bring the sauce to a boil, whisking the whole time, then turn the heat to low and simmer for 10 minutes. Remove the shallot halves (do not throw them out—those are for you to eat because you have earned some gravy-poached shallots in your life) and put the gravy in one of those awesome gravy boats.

6. Carve the chicken into 10 pieces as you would break down a chicken (see pages 4 to 5), and serve it with the gravy and sides, saying thanks to whatever god or gods created gravy.

Dangerously Crispy Spatchcocked Chicken

Serves 4 to 8, with lots of sauce left over for your
weeknight dinners (see page 55) or sandwich party (see page 104)

1 tablespoon kosher salt

1 tablespoon cornstarch

2 tablespoons vegetable oil

One 3- to 4-pound
(1.4 to 1.8kg) chicken,
spatchcocked as on page 6

1 tablespoon unsalted butter

12 sprigs fresh thyme

3 sprigs fresh rosemary

Contrary to my suspicions, it turns out spatchcocking a chicken is not just
a pathetic attempt to exert dominance over nature. Removing the chicken's
back so the bird lies flat gets you a super-crispy and beautiful whole-roasted
chicken in well under an hour. There is one important caveat: For the crispiest
skin, it's a two-step cooking process (still done in under an hour!)—you'll lay
the spatchcocked chicken skin-side *down* in a large sauté pan to get it started,
then put it in a super-hot oven to finish roasting. To maximize crispiness, do
what my old boss, Jean-Georges Vongerichten, does and put some cornstarch
on the skin. With the time saved on chicken roasting, make a fun sauce to serve
with it, like any of the suggested ideas on page 101. Crispy roast chicken and
fun sauce is already a pretty ideal dinner to make for your friends, but you can
serve it with the Chopped Chicken Salad with Watermelon & Ricotta Salata
(page 32), and that would be an awesome, deeply chickeny party.

1. Heat the oven to 500°F (260°C). In a small bowl, mix together the salt and
cornstarch. Sprinkle the mixture over the chicken skin and pat it in an even
layer. In a large ovenproof sauté pan, heat the oil over high heat until smoking.
Hold the chicken by the legs and shake off any excess cornstarch before gently
placing it, skin-side down, in the pan. Give the pan a careful but firm shake
to make sure your chicken doesn't stick. Cook the chicken on the stove for
10 minutes, checking occasionally to make sure the skin is caramelizing but
not burning.

2. Once you've achieved a light brown color, turn off the stove and place the
pan with the chicken in the oven. Roast it for 35 to 45 minutes, remove the pan
from the oven, and turn the oven to its broiler setting. Add the butter and herbs
to the pan and swirl it around until the butter is melted and the herbs are wilted,
about 2 minutes. Using tongs and a great deal of confidence, flip the chicken
over in the pan and put it back in the oven to broil for 2 to 3 minutes more, until
the skin is dark and so crispy that you're nervous it might hurt somebody's
mouth. Transfer the chicken to a plate and let it rest for 10 minutes before
carving and serving with one or more of the sauces on page 101. Warn your
guests about how crispy the skin is.

So Many Sauces, So Little Time!

Stovetop Super Salsa

In a small saucepan, combine 1 cup (240ml) water; 1 beefsteak tomato or a few plum tomatoes, roughly cut into 1- to 2-inch (2.5 to 5cm) chunks; 2 heads (about 24 cloves) garlic; 1 Fresno chile, halved lengthwise; ½ yellow onion, cut into a few pieces; a 1-inch (2.5cm) piece of ginger, sliced thinly against the grain; and ½ tablespoon kosher salt. Bring to a boil over high heat and boil for 10 minutes. Transfer to a blender and puree until smooth. This one is great hot or cold!

Green Goddess Dressing

In a blender, combine ½ cup (120ml) vegetable oil, ½ cup (120ml) buttermilk, ¼ cup (55g) mayonnaise, 4 sprigs dill (stems and leaves), 4 sprigs parsley (stems and leaves), 2 sprigs mint (stems and leaves), 1 tablespoon drained capers, 1 tablespoon freshly squeezed lemon juice, 1 garlic clove, and ½ teaspoon kosher salt. Puree until smooth.

Tangy Hoisin Barbecue Sauce

In a blender, combine ½ cup (120ml) soy sauce, ½ cup (115g) hoisin sauce, ¼ cup (75g) oyster sauce, 1 garlic clove, 2 tablespoons white wine vinegar, and ¼ red onion. Puree until smooth.

Pecan Romesco Sauce

In a blender, combine 2 red bell peppers, roasted (canned or jarred is perfectly fine), ½ cup (50g) toasted pecans, 1 Fresno chile, 4 sprigs cilantro (stems and leaves), 2 tablespoons extra-virgin olive oil, 1 tablespoon sherry vinegar, 1 tablespoon maple syrup, 1 teaspoon kosher salt, ¼ teaspoon smoked paprika, and 1 garlic clove. Puree until smooth.

Apricot-Basil Puree

Heat the broiler to its highest setting. In a small mixing bowl, combine 6 fresh apricots, halved, stems and pits removed, with 1 tablespoon extra-virgin olive oil. Toss to coat the fruit with the oil. Lay them out on a sheet pan, cut-side up, and broil for 3 to 5 minutes, or until the apricots are well caramelized on top. Transfer them to a food processor and add ¼ cup (60ml) extra-virgin olive oil, 10 leaves fresh basil, 1 tablespoon balsamic vinegar, ½ tablespoon kosher salt, ½ teaspoon dried oregano, and ¼ teaspoon red pepper flakes. Process until fairly smooth but still chunky.

Grilled Romaine Caesar Salad with Fried Chicken Croutons

Serves 4 as an appetizer

Spicy Caesar Dressing

2 egg yolks

8 anchovy fillets (optional)

1 garlic clove

2 tablespoons freshly squeezed lemon juice

1 tablespoon extra-virgin olive oil

1 teaspoon each Dijon mustard and gochujang

½ teaspoon kosher salt

Fried Chicken Croutons

1½ cups (90g) panko bread crumbs

Kosher salt

1 tablespoon sesame seeds

1 teaspoon fennel seeds

½ teaspoon each dried oregano and dried thyme

3 tablespoons cornstarch

2 eggs

1 pound (450g) boneless, skinless chicken thighs

1½ cups (355ml) vegetable oil, for frying

2 romaine hearts

Kosher salt

Extra-virgin olive oil

½ small red onion

½ cup (50g) shaved Parmesan

Freshly ground black pepper

There's something so festive about Caeser salad! In this one, the lettuce has been grilled before being drenched in a creamy, spicy Caeser-style vinaigrette, giving it a radical, smoky edge; the croutons are made of chicken, because the only way to improve crunchy bread is to put delicious chicken in the middle of it; and, well, you can't really improve upon tons of cheese. Since you've already fired up the grill, channel your inner Peter Luger and throw on the biggest steak you can find to go with your awesome salad. Sitting outside with a couple of your closest friends, eating grilled salad and grilled steak—this is why you have a backyard in the first place, no?

1. To make the dressing, combine the egg yolks, anchovies (if using—omit salt if so), garlic, lemon juice, olive oil, mustard, gochujang, and salt in a blender and blend until fully emulsified and thick. Refrigerate until ready to use.

2. To make the croutons, in a mixing bowl, combine the panko, 2 teaspoons salt, the sesame seeds, fennel seeds, oregano, and thyme and mix well. In a separate bowl, combine the cornstarch and eggs and whisk thoroughly. Cut the chicken into 1-inch (2.5cm) cubes and season it with 1 teaspoon salt; then add it to the bowl with the egg mixture and toss well, coating each piece completely. Pull out a small handful of chicken, drain any excess liquid, and place in the panko mixture, breading it well on all sides. Transfer the breaded chicken to a large plate and repeat with the remainder.

3. Fire up a grill to the "surface of Venus" setting. In a 2-quart (1.9L) saucepan, heat the vegetable oil to about 350°F (175°C) using a thermometer to check the temperature before frying. Fry the chicken in four batches, adjusting the stove to maintain 350°F (175°C). Drain the chicken croutons on a paper towel–lined plate and season with a little extra salt while they're still hot.

4. Halve the romaine hearts lengthwise and season with salt and olive oil on the cut side. Grill, cut-side down, until the edges are charred but the lettuce is still primarily raw, about 5 minutes. Meanwhile, slice the red onion thinly into rings.

5. Divide the grilled lettuce among four plates, cut-side up, and top each with some dressing, a handful of chicken croutons, Parmesan, several rings of red onion, and a pinch of black pepper, and serve.

CHICKEN SANDWICHES TO SERVE YOUR FRIENDS AND BE VERY POPULAR

I wrote a whole book full of sandwiches once; please don't expect me to do it again! Use this chart to come up with your own ideas and stop freeloading. And get off my lawn! (Just kidding.) Actually, use this handy chart to put together an awesome chicken sandwich by picking something from each column and combining them to form Chicken Sandwich Voltron.

BREAD	CHICKEN	SAUCE	STUFF-INS	UNEXPECTED GUESTS
Sourdough	Roast chicken (see page 3)	All of the onions relish (see page 149)	Green apple, jicama, and radish matchsticks	Pickled red onions (see page 79), blueberries (see page 20), or tomatoes (see page 83)
Demi baguette	Grilled chicken breast (see page 20)	Harissa Kewpie mayo (see page 20)	Sliced tomatoes	
Pumpernickel/rye	Poached chicken (see page 7)	Gochujang	Lettuce/greens	Kimchi
Potato bun		Hoisin sauce	Sliced cooked beets	Bacon
Brioche	Chicken meatloaf (see page 39)	Jelly/jam	Sliced roasted peppers	Fish sauce
Whole-wheat/multigrain/seeded bread	Fried chicken (see page 61)	Onion gravy (see page 48)	Shredded carrots, cucumber, and daikon	Mung bean sprouts
Delicious white bread	Chicken schnitzel (see page 16)	Spicy Caesar dressing (see page 102)	Sliced avocado	Mashed potatoes
English muffin	Chicken confit (see page 83)	Maple-soy dipping sauce (see page 123)	Cabbage slaw (see page 39)	Fried garlic (see page 119)
	Meyer lemon chicken salad (see page 51)	Super stock (see page 128), as au jus	Grilled broccolini (see page 48)	Chicken confit fat (see page 83)
	Chicken sausage (see page 77)	Buttery apple jam (see page 119)		Rice Krispies

A FEW FAVORITE COMBOS

Sourdough + chicken meatloaf (page 39) +
harissa Kewpie mayo (page 20) + green apple,
jicama, and radish matchsticks + fried garlic

Demi baguette + meyer lemon chicken salad
(page 51) + gochujang + lettuce/greens + bacon

English muffin + chicken confit (page 83) +
hoisin sauce + shredded carrots, daikon, and
cucumber + mashed potatoes

Pumpernickel/rye + chicken sausage (page 77) +
spicy Caesar dressing (page 102) +
cabbage slaw (page 39) + Rice Krispies

Delicious white bread + fried chicken (page 61) +
buttery apple jam (page 119) + grilled broccolini
(page 48) + kimchi

Grilled Chicken with Jalapeño Yogurt Marinade

Serves 2 to 4

½ cup (120g) full-fat plain Greek yogurt

2 jalapeños, stemmed and cut into a few rough pieces

One ½-inch (1.3cm) piece ginger, peeled and sliced thinly against the grain

4 garlic cloves

2 tablespoons kosher salt

2 tablespoons freshly squeezed lemon juice

½ tablespoon extra-virgin olive oil

½ teaspoon cumin seeds

One 3- to 4-pound (1.4 to 1.8kg) chicken, spatchcocked as on page 6

Yogurt is so good for you! It's full of bacteria that can help you digest food and make your coat so shiny. Oh wait, you don't want a shiny coat and good digestion? Well then this recipe is perfect for you because after we marinate our chicken in yogurt, we're going to grill it and kill all of the bacteria before eating it, so it shouldn't have any effect on your coat. But dear, sweet Lord Randolph Henry Spencer-Churchill, this marinade will knock your socks off. For one, it's gloriously spicy (though you can use just one jalapeño or leave them out altogether) and tangy. But it's also perfect for a grilled chicken because it keeps the skin crispy, thanks to all the sugars and proteins in the yogurt. Because this chicken is spatchcocked, it can lie flat on the grill, making it much easier to get an even color and maximum crispiness on all of the skin. This chicken goes well with any sides you want—I would vote for potato salad and corn on the cob (both great ways to temper the heat).

1. In a blender, combine the yogurt, jalapeños, ginger, garlic, salt, lemon juice, oil, and cumin seeds and puree until smooth. Put the chicken in a large plastic container or ziplock freezer bag, pour the marinade over it, seal, and shake to completely coat the chicken. Marinate in the refrigerator, covered, for at least 4 hours or up to 24 hours.

2. Heat your grill to 450°F (230°C). (You thought I was going to make another joke about the heat but I'm not that predictable!)

3. Brush and oil the grill well and put the chicken, skin-side down, onto it. Cook the chicken for about 5 minutes, or until the skin has developed a golden-brown color, then flip the chicken onto the bone side. Cook for another 20 minutes or so, until the bones are well charred and the meat has visibly tightened and is starting to pull away from the bones of the drumsticks. Flip the chicken back onto its skin side and cook for another 5 to 10 minutes, being careful not to let the skin get too dark—you want nicely charred, crispy skin with some blackened bits, like the bottom of a good slice of pizza. Once the chicken is cooked (it will have reached 165°F /75°C), let it rest for 5 to 10 minutes before carving and serving.

Broiled Chicken Breasts with Asparagus Salad & Tarragon Puree

Serves 4

4 split chicken breasts (bone-in, skin-on), about 3 pounds (1.4kg)

½ tablespoon kosher salt

2 teaspoons extra-virgin olive oil

1 teaspoon freshly ground black pepper

Asparagus Salad

1 pound (450g) asparagus, tough parts of the stalk removed

1 cup (175g) cherry tomatoes, halved

½ small shallot, diced

1 tablespoon rice wine vinegar

1½ teaspoons kosher salt

1½ teaspoons extra-virgin olive oil

Tarragon Puree

2 small yellow squash, roughly chopped (about 4 cups/500g)

3 garlic cloves

1 tablespoon extra-virgin olive oil

1 teaspoon kosher salt

¾ cup (22g) fresh tarragon leaves

Dinner at my house is almost always a big pot of beans, a chunk of braised meat, a big pot of braised meat and beans, or anything else I can cook on the stove for a long time and ladle over rice. But sometimes I make dishes I like to call Stupid Restaurant Food, which comprise separate components (none of which are stew) that are plated like we are at a restaurant. This dish would definitely qualify as Stupid Restaurant Food, with a squash puree swooshed on the plate like a fancy chef would do ten years ago, and sliced chicken arranged on top of the swoosh, and salad piled up on top of that. None of this means it's better than a pot of stew, or that it's difficult to prepare—the chicken is super simple, and requires only a little seasoning before it goes in the oven. And as it cooks, make the salad and the puree and it should all come together at about the same time.

1. Heat the oven to 400°F (200°C), positioning the rack 4 to 6 inches from the broiler. Put the chicken in a roasting pan, skin-side up, and season with the salt, oil, and pepper. Roast the chicken for 30 minutes, then turn on the broiler setting and broil the chicken until the skin is dark brown and crispy, 3 to 5 minutes. Pull it from the oven and let it rest in the pan for 15 minutes.

2. To make the salad, place the asparagus in a large sauté pan, adding enough water to cover the entire bottom of the pan (usually about ¼ cup, or 60ml), and cook over high heat until the water has evaporated entirely. Transfer the asparagus to a mixing bowl; add the tomatoes, shallot, vinegar, salt, and oil; and mix well to combine.

3. To make the puree, in the same sauté pan over medium heat, combine the squash with the garlic, oil, and salt; cover; and cook, stirring occasionally until the squash is falling apart and the garlic is soft, 10 to 12 minutes. Transfer the squash to a blender, add the tarragon, and puree until smooth.

4. With a large serving spoon, dollop the puree on a plate at nine o'clock. Stick the spoon in the middle of the dollop and drag it in an arc across the plate from nine o'clock to about two o'clock. Remove the bones from the cooked chicken breasts and slice them into a few 1-inch-thick (2.5cm-thick) portions. Put one chicken breast in the middle of the plate and drape the asparagus salad over it. Repeat with the remaining puree, chicken, and asparagus. Now you have Stupid Restaurant Food!

Tangy Rose's Lime–Glazed Wings

Serves 6

Rose's Lime Glaze

1½ cups (355ml) Rose's lime juice (or 1 cup/240ml freshly squeezed lime juice and ½ cup/120ml honey)

1½ cups (355ml) water

1 head garlic, cloves peeled and smashed

2 to 3 Fresno chiles, stems removed, cut in a few chunks

3 tablespoons vegetable oil

2 teaspoons kosher salt

½ teaspoon ground nutmeg

Wings

4½ pounds (2kg) chicken wings, wingtips removed, drumettes and flats separated

⅓ cup (80ml) vegetable oil

2 teaspoons kosher salt

¾ cup (15g) cilantro leaves, chopped, for serving

Rose's lime juice is one of those things that people complain about because they think it's not as good as fresh lime juice. And sure, it is not good at acting as lime juice because it isn't really lime juice. It is tart and a little bit sweet and smells like magical candy. If you put a splash in a vodka soda, you might accidentally become the MLB American League Rookie of the Year, and you will need some chicken wings to celebrate! I find that Rose's lime juice makes a perfect glaze for grilled or fried things because it is tart and sweet and sticky, and chicken wings are no exception. I will warn you that the Fresno chiles in this recipe can make the sauce pretty spicy, so feel free to seed them or just use half the chiles specified. And if you don't have a grill or you are not MLB American League Rookie of the Year, you can cook these wings on a sheet pan in the oven. They will be different from the grilled version but equally delicious—just like Rose's lime juice!

1. To make the glaze, in a small saucepan over medium heat, combine the Rose's lime juice, water, garlic, chiles, oil, salt, and nutmeg and cook until the mixture reduces to a thick syrup, 20 to 25 minutes. Transfer to a blender and puree until smooth. Keep in the blender and set aside—the sauce may separate as you cook the wings, and you may need to blend it again to get it smooth before using.

2. Heat the grill on high to the temperature of an erupting volcano's interior, or your oven to 450°F (230°C). If cooking your wings in the oven, line a rimmed sheet pan with aluminum foil.

3. To prep the wings, in a large mixing bowl, combine the wings, oil, and salt and mix well so the wings are fully covered.

4. Put the wings on the grill and cook for 20 to 25 minutes, or until they are cooked through and nicely charred (you might have to do this in a few batches). I like mine on the super well-done side. To cook in the oven, arrange the wings on the prepared sheet pan and bake for 35 to 45 minutes or until crisp and golden brown, flipping once after about 20 minutes.

5. Toss the cooked wings in a large mixing bowl with the Rose's lime glaze. Arrange on a platter, sprinkle with cilantro, and serve.

Chicken to Eat
When You Are Sad

My Grandmother's Chicken Noodle Soup (as Prepared by Her Daughter-in-Law, with Tweaks by the Grandson She Never Knew)

Serves 8

One 3- to 4-pound
(1.4 to 1.8kg) chicken

3 large carrots, peeled
and cut into thirds

1 parsnip, peeled
and quartered

4 whole cloves

1 medium yellow onion,
peeled and cut in half,
root and stem still
attached

10 sprigs parsley, stems
and leaves separated

3 tablespoons kosher salt

12 cups (2.8L) water

1 pound (450g) dried
egg noodles

My family's kitchen smelled like this soup at least once a month for my entire childhood. My mother learned the recipe from my father's mother, Clara, who came to the United States from Hungary in the 1930s and passed before I was born. It's the simplest chicken soup recipe, but also the chickeniest. And as with many oral family recipes, we all make it differently. Grandma Clara was quite fond of putting chicken feet in the broth, which apparently made it more yellow, as well as giblets for flavor and nutrition. My mom likes to add a bouillon cube or two at the end, but if you season generously along the way, that's not necessary (sorry, Mom!). My mother and grandmother both would serve a large platter with the chicken used to make the broth and all of the super-cooked vegetables alongside a few bowls of broth and noodles (almost like French pot-au-feu), and now I do that, too. My mom also butters saltine crackers to dip in her soup, which always seemed like a very-my-mom thing to do, but give it a try because it is delicious.

1. In a large pot, combine the chicken, carrots, and parsnip. Push 2 cloves into each onion half because that is how my mom does it and it looks cool. Put the onion halves in the pot, along with the parsley stems, salt, and water. Check out the level of the water in the pot. Turn the heat to high, bring to a boil, turn the heat to medium-low, and simmer the soup for 60 to 90 minutes, adding a little water as needed to keep the level about the same throughout cooking.

2. After an hour, using a slotted spoon and a pair of tongs, gently remove the chicken from the broth and place it on a large plate to cool. Remove the veggies as well and put them on a separate platter, discarding the parsley stems. Pull the cloves out of the onion halves and trim the stem end from each half with a paring knife. When everything has cooled a bit, shred the chicken, discarding the skin and bones, and cut the vegetables into ½-inch (1.3cm) pieces.

3. Cook the noodles according to the package directions. Put some cooked noodles into each bowl. Ladle over some broth and garnish with the parsley leaves. Serve the platter of veggies and chicken to be eaten with or in the soup, and make sure to have plenty of saltines and room-temperature butter on the table for dipping!

Savory Chicken Oatmeal with Braised Greens

Serves 4

2 cups (480ml) chicken stock

2 cups (480ml) whole milk

1 cup (160g) steel-cut oats

½ teaspoon kosher salt

Braised Greens

4 ounces (115g) sliced bacon, cut into ½-inch (1.3cm) strips

4 garlic cloves, smashed

¼ cup (60ml) chicken stock

1 pound (450g) Swiss chard, leaves and stems chopped into 1-inch (2.5cm) ribbons

2 teaspoons low-sodium soy sauce

1 teaspoon vegetable oil

1 teaspoon light brown sugar

1 teaspoon freshly squeezed lemon juice

1 teaspoon kosher salt

1 cup (170g) shredded cooked chicken (see page 7)

Unsalted butter or chicken confit fat (see page 83), for serving

Savory oatmeal. Do people think that's weird? If you think savory oats are weird, I suggest that you just get over it and try this recipe! Meaty chicken stock and a little creaminess from milk make plain ol' oats taste rich and borderline gluttonous, even though they are the absolute opposite. And though the dish doesn't need it, adding a little butter (or better yet, a little bit of the fat from chicken confit) while you're cooking the oats will make them so delicious that you'll probably have to leave town before the local townsfolk storm your house with pitchforks and torches . . . because they'll think you've created a monster of flavor. No? Sorry. Anyway, the oatmeal is great on its own, but piling on a sort of salad of gently braised greens and brown-sugary chicken (it works like pancakes and bacon with maple syrup) will make you a better, more understanding person, even if the townsfolk don't get it.

1. In a saucepan over medium-high heat, bring the stock and milk to a boil. Stir in the oats and salt. Lower the heat and simmer, stirring occasionally, until the mixture thickens up to the consistency of risotto and the oats are cooked but still chewy, 25 to 30 minutes.

2. While the oats are cooking, make the braised greens. Heat the bacon and garlic in a large sauté pan over medium heat. Cook, stirring occasionally, until the bacon and garlic are both browned, 8 to 10 minutes. Add the stock and half of the Swiss chard and cook, stirring and flipping the greens until they are about half their original size, 7 to 10 minutes. Add the rest of the chard, along with the soy sauce, oil, brown sugar, lemon juice, and salt and cook until the chard is completely wilted but still bright green and the stem pieces are tender and delicious but still vibrant and red, 3 to 5 minutes. Add the chicken and sauté for a few more minutes to heat through.

3. Divide the oatmeal among four bowls, top each one with a quarter of the greens and chicken mixture, add a pat of butter or 1 teaspoon of chicken confit fat if you're feeling ready to defend yourself against pitchforks, and serve.

Chicken Toast with Buttery Apple Jam

Serves 1 (with enough of the trickier components left over to make it a few more times)

Buttery Apple Jam

½ cup (110g) unsalted butter

1 tablespoon water

1 Golden Delicious (or similar) apple, not peeled or cored, chopped into 1-inch (2.5cm) cubes

1 Bosc pear, not peeled or cored, chopped into 1-inch (2.5cm) cubes

1 teaspoon honey

Fried Garlic

¼ cup (60ml) vegetable oil

½ head garlic, cloves peeled

1 boneless, skinless chicken breast, cut into ¼-inch-thick (6mm-thick) strips

½ teaspoon kosher salt

1 lime, peeled and sectioned to remove the pith and membranes

⅛ red onion, thinly sliced

¼ cup (30g) thinly sliced radishes

4 sprigs fresh dill, fronds only

2 slices crusty bread

Freshly ground black pepper

When I'm feeling meh, I just eat toast, one of the easiest things to make. Because I grew up in New York State, apples are a go-to topping for toast, as is chicken (see page 51, page 138, and, heck, page 149!)—so, I thought, why not combine them? As always, I wanted some acidity. While apples often get tossed with lemon juice to prevent oxidation, lime juice sounded more festive. And limes and chicken make me think of pho ga. And Vietnamese food, chicken, and limes make me think of herbs, radishes, and fried garlic. So I put them together on toast and ate it while watching the movie *The Outsiders* on TV, which is *almost* as good as the book.

1. Heat the oven to 300°F (150°C).

2. To make the jam, melt the butter with the water in a small saucepan over low heat. Add the apple, pear, and honey; increase the heat to medium low; and cook for 30 to 40 minutes. Set a food mill or fine-mesh sieve over a baking dish, and mill or sieve the mixture. Put the dish in the oven and bake for 1½ to 2½ hours, until the jam is all a rich caramel color and the butter separates. Transfer this to a metal bowl and refrigerate for 30 minutes, whisking every 5 minutes, until the mixture reemulsifies (this step is nonnegotiable!). You may need to add a couple tablespoons of hot water to help reemulsify it.

3. To fry the garlic, heat the oil in a small, high-sided saucepan to 350°F (175°C). Thinly slice the garlic lengthwise. Fry until golden, about 5 minutes. Strain through a fine-mesh sieve over a heatproof container, reserving the oil. Transfer the garlic to a paper towel–lined plate.

4. In a sauté pan over high heat, heat 2 teaspoons of the reserved garlic oil until smoking. Add the chicken to the pan in an even layer. Season it with the salt and cook, undisturbed, 5 to 7 minutes, until it's mostly white but a little pink in the middle. Stir and continue cooking until it's completely white, another minute. Transfer to a bowl and add the lime, 1 tablespoon of the fried garlic, the red onion, radishes, dill, and 1 teaspoon garlic oil, tossing well.

5. Toast the bread and spread some jam on each slice. Top with the chicken mixture, more fried garlic, and some pepper. The remaining jam and garlic oil can be refrigerated for up to 1 month, and the fried garlic keeps for months in an airtight container on the counter/in the pantry.

Chickeny White Beans & Wilted Romaine

Serves 4

2 teaspoons extra-virgin olive oil, plus more for drizzling

2 whole chicken legs (thighs and drumsticks), 1½ pounds (680g)

1 head garlic, cloves smashed

2 cups (480ml) chicken stock (see page 8)

1½ cups (390g) cooked cannellini beans, plus ⅓ cup (80ml) cooking liquid (or one 15-ounce/ 425g can cannellini beans, no salt added, drained and with canning liquid reserved)

2 teaspoons kosher salt

1 head romaine lettuce, roughly chopped

1 ounce (30g) Parmesan, grated

1 lemon, cut into 8 wedges, for serving

This is an adaptation of escarole and white beans, a dish that is so perfect that it needn't be improved upon. And I wouldn't presume to say that I did here—this is just different! Reduce chicken stock with bean broth to create a sticky, awesome glaze; braise chicken legs in the broth before it reduces to get it super fortified; and then toss in some shredded romaine lettuce right at the end because it won't need a lot of time in the pan like escarole would. The romaine brings some bright-colored, slightly crunchy contrast to an otherwise all-braised dish. Serve this with crusty bread to sop up the broth, and I challenge you to be sad. Or take the chicken meat off the bone, shred it, and use it as a ragu for pasta, and your family will stop worrying so much about you.

1. In a large sauté pan with high sides, heat the oil over medium-high heat until smoking. Add the chicken legs, skin-side down. Cook until well browned, 6 to 8 minutes, flip, and cook until the other side is well browned, another 6 to 8 minutes. Turn the heat to low and add the garlic, stirring and cooking until browned, 6 to 8 minutes more. Add the stock, bean cooking liquid, and salt and increase the heat to high. When the mixture comes to a boil, turn the heat to low and cook until the chicken legs are super tender and the liquid has reduced by half, 40 to 55 minutes.

2. Add the beans and simmer for 10 minutes, or until they look nicely glazed. Increase the heat to medium and add the lettuce. Stir until the lettuce is wilted and the chicken is hot again. Divide the chicken legs into two. Then ladle the stew into bowls, top with a piece of chicken along with some Parmesan and a little drizzle of oil, and serve with lemon wedges.

Bean Rules for Beans That Rule

1. When cooking dried beans from scratch, don't worry about soaking them beforehand. They will be just as tender if you cook them without soaking first.

2. Be cautious with the amount of liquid you're using to cook your beans, maintaining a ratio of 6 cups (1.4L) of liquid to 1 cup (160g) of dried beans. It's much easier to add water than to cook it off.

3. I am not a believer in al dente beans, so I recommend you cook them until they aren't the least bit crunchy—even if this means some are falling apart while others are still cooking. The overly creamy beans will make your sauce better.

Chicken & Scallion Waffles with Maple-Soy Dipping Sauce

Makes 4 to 6 waffles

¾ cup (95g) all-purpose flour

¾ cup (105g) rice flour

¼ cup (35g) cornstarch

1½ teaspoons kosher salt

1 teaspoon baking powder

½ teaspoon each freshly ground black pepper and dried thyme

1 egg white

1¼ cups (300ml) water

1 tablespoon vegetable oil

1½ teaspoons each low-sodium soy sauce and gochujang

8 ounces (225g) boneless, skinless chicken breast, cut into ½-inch (1.3cm) chunks

1 cup (115g) mung bean sprouts

½ small zucchini, coarsely grated

½ bunch scallions, white and green parts, thinly sliced

Maple-Soy Dipping Sauce

2 tablespoons each low-sodium soy sauce and maple syrup

1 tablespoon unsalted butter, plus more for serving

2 teaspoons freshly squeezed lemon juice

¼ teaspoon red pepper flakes

Mixing together a batter and griddling it is one of the best ways I can think of to cheer myself up. But I so rarely want to eat something that is just sweet or just savory, so I often need a transitional object, like chicken and waffles, to satisfy me (not unlike my daughter's penguin security blanket, but a little bit crispier and stickier—though her penguin security blanket is decidedly a little crispy and sticky, too). This dish is technically chicken and waffles, in that it involves both chicken and waffles! But it's more like pajeon, a savory Korean pancake that often contains seafood and vegetables and is eaten with a tangy and slightly sweet dipping sauce. These chicken waffles are fairly crispy when they come out of the waffle iron, and thus are best enjoyed right away, but you could easily warm and crisp up leftovers in a 400°F (200°C) oven. I suggest you make a nice big salad, whip up a pitcher of mimosas, heat up the dipping sauce, and then just start making waffles and eating them as they come out. Alternatively, these waffles are equally delicious eaten cold, directly out of the fridge, in a bathrobe while halfway watching the film *Taken* and playing Candy Crush on your phone later that night.

1. In a large mixing bowl, whisk together the flours, cornstarch, salt, baking powder, black pepper, and thyme. In a separate bowl, whisk together the egg white, water, oil, soy sauce, and gochujang. Pour the wet ingredients over the dry ingredients and whisk just until combined. Add the chicken, bean sprouts, zucchini, and scallions and stir until fully combined.

2. Heat a waffle iron, coat it with cooking spray, and put in about 1¼ cups (300ml) of batter, or enough to fill your waffle iron, for each waffle. Cook the waffles until they're nicely browned and crispy, 5 to 7 minutes (a few minutes longer for larger irons).

3. To make the dipping sauce, while the first waffle is cooking, combine the soy sauce, maple syrup, butter, lemon juice, and red pepper flakes in a small saucepan over medium heat. Cook just long enough to melt the butter. This sauce won't stay emulsified, so you'll have to stir it every once in a while.

4. Serve the waffles with a pat of butter and the dipping sauce drizzled over the top (plus extra on the side, for dunking).

Chicken & Black-Eyed Pea Stew with Smoked Paprika

Serves 4

2 tablespoons
vegetable oil

4 bone-in chicken thighs,
about 1½ pounds (680g)

1 head garlic (10 to
12 cloves), peeled
and smashed

1 tablespoon
smoked paprika

One tomato, cored and
chopped into ½-inch
(1.3cm) chunks

1 jalapeño, stemmed,
seeded, and sliced into
¼-inch (6mm) rounds

4 ounces (115g) dried
black-eyed peas
(about ½ cup)

4 cups (950ml) water,
plus more as needed

½ tablespoon kosher salt

½ tablespoon
peanut butter

Cooked rice, for serving

Chopped cilantro (stems
and leaves), for serving

Lime wedges, for serving

To me, chicken and beans in the same pot feels like the very definition of cooking. So if it were up to me, this book would have been called *Chicken & Beans: Tokyo Drift* and would have been full of beans cooked in chicken stock and chicken cooked in bean stock and photos of fast cars and faster stoves. But it's not, so we'll make do with this awesome chicken and bean recipe instead. Simmering chicken thighs and black-eyed peas with a few aromatics pulls an immense amount of starch from the beans and flavor out of the chicken to create a magnificent sauce. The beans get super tender, and the chicken nearly falls apart. Black-eyed peas are an especially nutty, savory, earthy kind of bean that cooks quickly, but they can be strong-flavored, so I won't be offended if you switch them out for pintos or black beans. This stew is heaven served over rice with chopped cilantro and a squeeze of lime juice, but it is just as good unadorned, with just a spoon and a cold beer.

1. In a large ovenproof sauté pan with high sides, or a Dutch oven, heat the oil over high heat until smoking, then add the chicken thighs, skin-side down. Cook for 7 to 10 minutes, or until the skin is a deep and beautiful brown and the oil has spattered all over the stove (I'm sorry, but this will be worth it, I promise!). Flip the chicken, add the garlic, and cook for 3 to 4 minutes more, or until the garlic is dark brown. Add the smoked paprika, stirring it into the fat in the pan, and then add the tomato and jalapeño. Next, add the beans, water, salt, and peanut butter and stir well to combine. Bring to a boil, turn the heat to low, and simmer.

2. Cook the stew for 45 minutes, or until the beans are tender, stirring occasionally and basting the chicken skin from time to time, making sure that beans don't end up on top of the chicken thighs or they won't cook properly. Add water to maintain a level that is saucy but doesn't come up over the tops of the chicken thighs.

3. Heat the broiler to its highest setting. Put the whole pot about 6 inches (15cm) under the broiler and broil for 3 to 5 minutes, or until the skin on the chicken thighs is crispy and dark. Serve over rice with a handful of chopped cilantro and a squeeze of lime juice.

Coconut Milk Chicken à la King

Serves 4

Sweet Potato Wedges

2 large sweet potatoes, 1½ to 2 pounds (680 to 900g), peeled and cut into ½-inch (1.3cm) wedges

1 tablespoon vegetable oil

½ teaspoon kosher salt

Chicken à la King

1 tablespoon vegetable oil

5 garlic cloves, smashed

½ yellow onion, cut into ¼-inch (6mm) slices

1 jalapeño, stemmed, halved, unseeded, and sliced into ¼-inch (6mm) half-moons

2 cups (140g) sliced button or cremini mushrooms

1 tablespoon kosher salt

½ teaspoon dried thyme

½ teaspoon freshly ground black pepper

¼ teaspoon ground allspice

⅛ teaspoon ground nutmeg

One 13.5-ounce (400ml) can coconut milk

1 tablespoon cornstarch

1 pound (450g) boneless, skinless chicken breasts or thighs, thinly sliced

1 cup (140g) English peas, fresh or frozen and thawed

Chicken à la King is one of those recipes with a contested history, and I think that is so fun. According to the internet, it was invented in the late nineteenth century either by the chef of Delmonico's or one of a few different hotel chefs in New York City or London or possibly Philadelphia. But regardless of its origin story, it generally involves diced chicken and vegetables cooked in a creamy béchamel sauce, and it kind of resembles chicken potpie filling. This version is as creamy as the original, but it gets that creaminess from coconut milk and a little bit of cornstarch. Yes, this dish is dairy- and gluten-free, but it also feels approachable enough that it can hang out with your other friends without being awkward and shy. The nutmeg, allspice, and pepper flavoring this dish boldly add complexity to the creamy chicken. Serve it with sweet potato wedges on the side and your day will get better.

1. Heat the oven to 400°F (200°C) with a roasting pan or sheet pan in it.

2. To make the potato wedges, in a medium mixing bowl, toss the sweet potato wedges with the oil and salt. Carefully pull out the sheet pan and spread the sweet potatoes onto it in a single layer. Roast for 20 minutes, flip the sweet potatoes, and roast for another 15 minutes, or until they are dark brown and tender.

3. While the sweet potato wedges are baking, make the chicken. In a large saucepan or Dutch oven, heat the oil and garlic over medium heat until the garlic just starts to caramelize, 2 to 3 minutes. Add the onion, jalapeño, mushrooms, salt, thyme, pepper, allspice, and nutmeg and cook, stirring, for 10 minutes, or until the vegetables are soft and the onion is becoming translucent.

4. In a small mixing bowl, combine 1 cup (240ml) of the coconut milk and the cornstarch and stir until the cornstarch is fully dissolved. Add the slurry to the saucepan, stirring constantly. Increase the heat to high, still stirring constantly, and bring the mixture to a boil, yes, stirring constantly. Lower the heat to a simmer, add the chicken, and cook for 7 to 10 minutes, or until the chicken is no longer pink and the sauce has glazed everything nicely. Turn off the heat and stir in the peas. If it looks like it's getting too dry, add a splash of the remaining coconut milk so that the sauce coats all of the ingredients and there is a little extra in the pan.

5. Serve the chicken with the sweet potato wedges on the side.

Braised Chicken Ramen in Super Stock

Serves 2

2 teaspoons vegetable oil

2 bone-in chicken thighs, about ¾ pound (340g)

1 strip bacon, standard cut

4 cups (950ml) chicken stock

1 large onion, unpeeled and thinly sliced

1 russet potato, unpeeled, sliced crosswise into ¼-inch (6mm) rounds

One 1-inch (2.5cm) piece ginger, unpeeled and thinly sliced

1 large piece konbu, about 5 by 5 inches (13 by 13cm)

1 tablespoon dry vermouth

2 packages instant ramen (chicken flavor, of course)

½ bunch scallions, white and green parts, thinly sliced

Soft-boiled egg (see page 53); cooked corn kernels, cut off the cob; raw spinach or arugula; or raw mung bean sprouts (optional)

1 lime, cut into wedges

When I first heard that there was a super-hip, new restaurant in New York City serving ramen noodles, it blew my mind that the dried packs of noodle soup I had grown up with were related to a wildly popular food trend. Turns out it wasn't quite like that, but I still prefer the grocery-store noodles anyway, especially when they're cooked in an awesome homemade broth. The broth for this chicken ramen is a fortified chicken stock that borrows a few tricks from dashi, a savory, aromatic Japanese broth made by steeping water with bonito flakes (smoked, dried, and thinly shaved tuna) and konbu (a dried kelp that has a ton of glutamic acid—that's *umami* to you). Use this broth for any number of things, but if you're going to make ramen with it, you'd be a fool not to also include the flavor packet that comes with the noodles. If you don't use it, be sure to send it to me, care of Food52. I will put it to good use by seasoning a roast chicken or cucumber salad.

1. In a stockpot, heat the oil over high heat until it is smoking. Add the chicken thighs, skin-side down, turn the heat to medium, and cook until nicely browned, 7 to 10 minutes. Flip and cook the other side until browned, 7 to 10 minutes. Add the bacon, stock, onion, potato, ginger, konbu, and vermouth; bring the mixture to a boil over high heat; turn the heat to low; and simmer the stock. After about 10 minutes, remove the konbu, discarding it or reserving it to chop up and put back in the soup later.

2. Continue to cook the thighs in the stock for another 35 minutes, or until tender, maintaining a consistent level of liquid (about 4 cups/950ml) by adding water as necessary.

3. Strain the super-stock through a medium-mesh sieve, setting aside the chicken thighs.

4. Return the stock to the pot, bringing it to a boil, then add the packaged dried noodles and cook for 2 minutes. Meanwhile, if you reserved your konbu, chop it up finely. When the noodles are cooked, add either 1 flavor packet or 2 teaspoons salt, throw in the chopped konbu, and stir well to incorporate. Shred the chicken thighs and discard the skin and bones. Divide the pulled meat, noodles, and broth among two soup bowls. Top with the scallions, along with any of the topping options listed in the ingredient list (I love a soft-boiled egg and a handful of arugula). Serve with lime wedges on the side.

Creamy Chicken Baked Pasta with Cabbage

Serves 6 to 8

6 garlic cloves

2 pounds (900g) boneless, skinless chicken thighs

One 28-ounce (794g) can crushed tomatoes

1 cup (240ml) heavy cream

½ head savoy cabbage, finely shredded

8 ounces (225g) mild Gouda, shredded

1 pound (450g) rotelle or other short pasta shape, cooked in boiling water for three-fourths of the time instructed (7 to 9 minutes)

1½ tablespoons kosher salt

1 cup (60g) panko bread crumbs

2 tablespoons unsalted butter, melted

You know how after you've just flown a manned mission to Mars and discovered not only signs of extraterrestrial life but *actual* extraterrestrial life, and they're like, "Wow, are you Tyler Kord? We *loved* your sandwich book," and then they give you a gift, but you can't show it to anybody yet because they said that mankind isn't ready to have this kind of power, and so you come home and hide all kinds of clues about it in a cookbook about chicken, and then you're just so tired that you want to make something super-hands-off for dinner? This recipe is that. The chicken, savoy cabbage, and cheesy, tomatoey sauce all really come together in the oven, and the par-cooked pasta soaks up just enough of it to make a creamy, sturdy casserole. You can use any pasta shape you'd like (spaceship-shaped?), though I like rotelle, or wagon wheel–shaped pasta, because it really holds onto the chickeny, cabbagey sauce.

1. Heat the oven to 425°F (220°C).

2. In a food processor, process the garlic until it is well chopped. Add the chicken and pulse until there are no chunks larger than ½ inch (1.3cm). (You could also chop both the garlic and chicken by hand.)

3. Transfer the chopped chicken and garlic to a large mixing bowl; add the tomatoes, heavy cream, cabbage, Gouda, cooked pasta, and salt; and mix very well. Scoop everything into a 9 by 13-inch (23 by 33cm) casserole dish and spread out the mixture evenly.

4. In a small bowl, mix together the panko and the melted butter and sprinkle over the top of the casserole. Cover the casserole with a couple pieces of aluminum foil. Bake, covered, for 30 minutes, then remove the foil and bake, uncovered, for 15 minutes, or until the casserole is piping hot and smells amazing. I hope you are ready for this kind of power.

Dishes to Get Your Picky Kids to Eat Real Food, Chicken Edition

---

Chicken Spiedies,
aka Righteous Chicken on a Bun

Serves 4

1/3 cup (80ml) vegetable oil

1/4 cup (60ml) freshly squeezed lemon juice

1/4 cup (60ml) distilled white vinegar

2 garlic cloves

2 sprigs fresh mint

2 sprigs fresh dill

1/2 tablespoon kosher salt

1 teaspoon low-sodium soy sauce

1 teaspoon garlic powder

1 teaspoon freshly ground black pepper

1/2 teaspoon dried oregano

1/4 teaspoon red pepper flakes

1/4 teaspoon ground cardamom

1 1/2 pounds (680g) boneless, skinless chicken breasts or thighs, cut into 1-inch (2.5cm) chunks

4 super-soft hero rolls, split lengthwise

Shredded iceberg lettuce, chopped tomatoes, chopped white onion, sliced pepperoncini, and chopped olives

It was at a summertime fair in my hometown of Ithaca, New York, that young Tyler, a professionally picky eater who really just wanted to eat plain cold cuts on plain white bread, discovered something perfect: chicken that tasted like it had been marinated in Italian dressing, skewered and grilled over charcoal, and put onto a soft, white bun with absolutely nothing else on it. A chicken spiedie. This was during a time when I didn't bring up food in conversation lest I be forced to try something unappealing, so I got to eat spiedies only once a year at the festival. Had I just spoken up, I would've discovered that spiedies were all around me, I just didn't know where to look. They're so popular near where I grew up that there's an annual Spiedie Fest & Balloon Rally in nearby Binghamton! This recipe takes my favorite parts of several versions and throws some curveballs: mint and dill for brightness, and ground cardamom for an air of mystery. Spiedies make me heart New York more than ever! Was that cheesy or amazing? I'm going with both.

1. In a blender, combine the oil, lemon juice, vinegar, garlic, mint, dill, salt, soy sauce, garlic powder, black pepper, oregano, red pepper flakes, and cardamom and puree until smooth and emulsified.

2. Put the chicken in a large mixing bowl and pour the marinade over it, reserving about 1/2 cup marinade in a small bowl, and covering and refrigerating it. Mix the chicken well with the marinade, cover, and refrigerate for at least 4 hours or up to 24. The acidic marinade will start to break down the chicken, so if a more tender texture bothers you, marinate for 4 to 5 hours. I, however, am a fan of that texture and think an aggressively long, 24-hour marinade gives the chicken that much more flavor.

3. Heat a grill until it is so hot you (almost) can't look directly at it. Skewer the chicken; you can make a giant skewer to save space or lots of little ones for easier turning. Cook the skewered chicken, turning three times, until nicely charred, 5 to 7 minutes on each of the four sides. Let the chicken rest for 10 minutes, then take it off the skewers.

4. To serve on the rolls, top with whichever of the following makes you the happiest: lettuce, tomatoes, onion, reserved marinade, pepperoncini, olives. *Or* don't use any toppings, as it's meant to be eaten, in my book (which this literally is).

Crispy Quinoa- & Millet-Breaded Chicken Fingers

Serves 4

3 teaspoons vegetable oil

½ cup (60g) quinoa flour

½ cup (60g) millet flour

1 tablespoon kosher salt

½ teaspoon smoked paprika

½ teaspoon dried oregano

½ cup (120ml) water

2 pounds (900g) boneless, skinless chicken breasts, sliced into 1-inch-wide (2.5cm-wide) strips, or 2 pounds (900g) chicken tenders

Dipping Sauce

½ bunch scallions, white and green parts, thinly sliced

½ cup (120g) sour cream

1 tablespoon nutritional yeast

2 teaspoons freshly squeezed lemon juice

½ teaspoon garlic powder

½ teaspoon kosher salt

When I think of chicken fingers, I like to picture chickens with hands on the ends of their wings composed of five huge strips of boneless meat that they use to high-five each other or play handball. But I realize that chickens probably don't have fingers like that (at least for now). Either way, I love chicken fingers. They're the elegant version of a chicken nugget, and are so good for dipping in things, unlike chicken nuggets, which put your (human) fingers at risk of getting sauced. These baked chicken fingers get a major flavor boost from their breading of ground quinoa and millet, both of which are nutty, sturdy, amazing grains in their own right. So while I'm not a (licensed) doctor, I'm pretty sure these will make you incredibly strong and good-looking, while also satisfying your craving for fried chicken, by providing a hearty, crunchy, and handheld way to eat poultry!

1. Drizzle 1½ teaspoons of the oil on a half sheet pan or in a large roasting pan and put it in the oven. Heat the oven to 450°F (230°C) with the pan inside.

2. In a mixing bowl, combine ¼ cup (30g) of the quinoa flour, ¼ cup (30g) of the millet flour, the salt, the remaining 1½ teaspoons oil, the smoked paprika, oregano, and water. Whisk the mixture together thoroughly. Add the chicken and stir until it's completely coated in the batter.

3. In a separate mixing bowl, combine the remaining ¼ cup (30g) quinoa flour and remaining ¼ cup (30g) millet flour and mix well. Transfer the coated chicken to this bowl, one piece at a time, and toss until the chicken is completely coated and all of the flour is absorbed. Set aside the breaded chicken on a large plate. Don't be afraid if the breading gets a little shaggy— that is where the crispiness will come from!

4. Pull the sheet pan out of the oven and arrange the breaded chicken on it in one layer. Bake the chicken for 10 minutes, flip every piece, and return it to the oven and bake for another 6 to 7 minutes. Turn on the oven's broiler setting, move the pan 6 inches (15cm) under the broiler, and broil for 3 to 5 minutes more, or until the chicken is nutty-brown in color and crispy and amazing.

5. To make the dipping sauce, while the chicken bakes, combine the scallions, sour cream, nutritional yeast, lemon juice, garlic powder, and salt and mix thoroughly.

6. Serve the chicken fingers with the dipping sauce.

Rosemary-Butter Chicken with Scrambled Eggs

Serves 4

½ cup (110g) unsalted butter

2 teaspoons kosher salt

4 sprigs fresh rosemary

12 sprigs fresh thyme

1 shallot, thinly sliced

1 boneless, skin-on chicken breast, about 8 ounces (225g)

6 eggs

4 slices crusty bread

Scrambled egg recipes seem silly, because what can be more simple than making scrambled eggs? And yet the internet is full of suggestions for them, from adding milk to whipping air into the eggs to my absolute least favorite, undercooking the eggs so they'll be "creamy." I am not worried about getting sick or anything—I just find scrambled eggs to be so much more delicious when they're fully cooked. All over the world you'll find eggs cooked forever in soups and stews: Jewish cholent, South Indian egg curry, or Cajun shrimp and egg stew. They involve no yolk porn but just super-delicious eggs. (If you've ever overcooked a hard-boiled egg, you'll know that eggs develop more of their distinctive eggy flavor the longer they're cooked—unpleasant aroma aside, an overcooked egg is a powerful thing.) This dish celebrates the well-cooked scrambled egg, bringing the creaminess with butter-poached chicken, and makes the question of which came first, or the usual photos of yolks oozing all over the place, seem entirely irrelevant.

1. In a small sauté pan over medium-low heat, combine the butter, 1 teaspoon of the salt, the rosemary, thyme, and shallot and stir until the butter melts. Add the chicken breast and poach in the butter sauce, flipping occasionally, for 15 to 20 minutes, or until firm to the touch. Remove the chicken from the pan and strain the butter into another container. Remove the skin and shred the chicken. It can be a little on the pink side now because it will finish cooking with the eggs.

2. Crack the eggs and remaining 1 teaspoon salt into a blender and buzz on low speed until uniformly smooth. You could also do this in a small container with an immersion blender.

3. In a large nonstick pan over medium heat, add the eggs, shredded chicken, and 2 tablespoons of the strained chicken butter. Cook, stirring only occasionally (we want nice big curds to form!), until the eggs are set, 3 to 6 minutes.

4. While the eggs are cooking, toast the bread on a hot grill pan or in the toaster to your desired toastiness level. Drizzle the remaining chicken butter on the toast and serve topped with the eggs.

Chicken Pilaf for Hungry Kids & People

Serves 4 as an entrée, 6 to 8 as a side

4 bone-in chicken thighs, about 1½ pounds (680g), skin removed

3 cups (710ml) chicken stock

1½ cups (270g) basmati rice

8 garlic cloves, smashed

2 tablespoons unsalted butter (or chicken confit fat, see page 83)

½ tablespoon kosher salt

1 teaspoon fennel seeds

½ teaspoon ground cardamom

2 bay leaves

½ cup (90g) orzo

One 5-ounce (140g) bag baby spinach

½ cup (70g) salted dry-roasted peanuts, finely chopped by hand or pulsed in a food processor

I could eat rice for every meal. When you add pasta to the mix, like in this pilaf, I am even more on board because I want every kind of starch in my mouth at all times. But don't worry, the basmati rice in this pilaf is fragrant and feathery; the spinach makes it feel virtuous; and the tender chicken just kind of melts into the dish, with the help of the chicken-stock cooking liquid, packing the pilaf with protein but letting the picky eaters in our lives feel like they're just eating a big bowl of the richest, meatiest, most transcendent rice out there. This pilaf is simple, familiar (can you say Rice-a-Roni?), and yet a little bit different (special shout-out to spinach and the humble peanut, which create a chard-and-pine-nut sort of vibe) from any of the existing and amazing rice pilaf recipes from around the world.

1. In a stockpot, combine the chicken thighs, stock, rice, garlic, butter, salt, fennel seeds, cardamom, and bay leaves. Bring the mixture to a boil over high heat, turn the heat to low, and simmer.

2. In a small sauté pan, toast the orzo over medium-high heat, stirring regularly, until lightly brown and fragrant, 5 to 7 minutes. Add the toasted orzo to the pot with the rice mixture (by now, it should have been cooking for about 15 minutes), give it a stir to combine, cover the pot with a lid, and let it cook, undisturbed, for 17 to 20 minutes, or until the stock is absorbed, the rice and pasta are tender, and the chicken is white and fully cooked through. Turn off the heat.

3. Add the spinach and peanuts to the pot, cover with the lid, and let it steam for 2 minutes, until the spinach is wilted. Remove the cover and stir until the peanuts are fully mixed into the pilaf. Remove and discard the bay leaves.

4. Remove the bones from the chicken thighs. Divide the pilaf among four plates, top each with a piece of chicken, and serve.

Chicken Burgers with Shallots & Ginger

Makes 4 quarter-pound burgers

1 pound (450g) ground chicken, or 1¼ pounds (570g) boneless, skinless skinless chicken thighs, for grinding

1 shallot, finely diced

One ½-inch (1.3cm) piece ginger, peeled and finely grated

1 tablespoon brown sugar

2 teaspoons kosher salt

¼ teaspoon toasted sesame oil

Jicama Slaw

1 small jicama, peeled and shredded

½ small red onion, thinly sliced

2 teaspoons freshly squeezed lemon juice

1 teaspoon extra-virgin olive oil

1 teaspoon kosher salt

To Serve

4 burger buns (I like Arnold country potato buns)

1 ripe avocado, peeled, pitted, and smashed

Why aren't chicken burgers a thing? They're lean, yes, but they're no leaner than turkey burgers, and they're much less lean than not eating any kind of burger at all. Also, they're stupid delicious, especially when grilled. For the best flavor and texture in these chicken burgers, I would definitely buy some boneless thighs and grind them yourself instead of buying preground chicken. I don't normally mix things into my burgers, but these work well with mix-ins of all sorts, especially ginger and shallots (just a hint, for an interesting but not super-intense flavor), a combination I stole from Chef Greg Brainin of Jean-Georges. He usually combines shallots and ginger with fresh ground tuna and the entire ocean stands still and salutes. When the ginger and shallot are mixed with chicken and grilled, the deep, charred aroma that results just screams summertime. And you can serve them as you would any other burger, or you can be adventurous and top them with smashed avocado and a crunchy jicama slaw. Get your kids to help you make the slaw so they are curious about what jicama is and want to try it on their burgers!

1. Cut the chicken into even 1-inch (2.5cm) pieces. Working in small batches, place the chicken in your food processor and pulse to finely chop, but avoid turning it into a mousse (which is good for some things, but not exactly what people have in mind for burgers!).

2. Heat the grill to hot as all get out. In a mixing bowl, combine the ground chicken, shallot, ginger, brown sugar, salt, and sesame oil and mix well. Divide the meat into four portions and form each into a patty that's 4½ to 5 inches (11.5 to 13cm) in diameter. Put the burgers on the grill and don't touch them until they are almost completely cooked through, about 5 minutes. Flip the burgers and finish cooking until no longer pink, 1 to 2 minutes more.

3. To make the slaw, in a mixing bowl, add the jicama, red onion, lemon juice, olive oil, and salt and toss well to combine.

4. To serve, toast the burger buns on the grill until warmed through and lightly browned, 15 to 20 seconds. Put one patty on each burger bun and divide the smashed avocado and slaw between the four burgers to top each of them.

Grapefruit & Rosemary Chicken

Serves 4

1 egg

2½ tablespoons cornstarch, plus ½ cup (80g)

2 teaspoons kosher salt

1½ pounds (680g) boneless, skinless chicken breasts or thighs, cut into 1-inch (2.5cm) chunks

½ cup (60g) all-purpose flour

1½ cups (360ml) vegetable oil, plus 2 tablespoons

6 cloves garlic, smashed

2 scallions, sliced into ¼-inch (6mm) rounds

1 tablespoon grapefruit zest, plus ⅓ cup (80ml) freshly squeezed grapefruit juice

3 tablespoons maple syrup

1 tablespoon distilled white vinegar

2 teaspoons fresh rosemary, minced

½ teaspoon cracked pink peppercorns

1 teaspoon toasted sesame oil

½ cup (120ml) chicken stock

Cooked quinoa, for serving

Steamed green beans, for serving

My absolute favorite breakfast on planet Earth is cold, leftover Chinese takeout. This morning I ate leftover shrimp with broccoli, and it had everything I needed to start my day right: protein, fiber, fat, and just a touch of sugar. I would choose that over Frosted Flakes any day of the week because my body is a glorious temple and it deserves the best. So we're channeling my breakfast preferences here, in the best, crispiest way, borrowing a technique from the American Chinese food classics, orange chicken and sesame chicken: We'll dredge and fry bite-size pieces of boneless, skinless chicken and then coat them in a juicy, slightly bitter, grapefruity sauce that's spiked with pink peppercorns and rosemary. And while it will have zero semblance of crunch tomorrow because of the sauce, it will still be so appropriate and delicious. You could serve this with some cooked quinoa and super crunchy, barely steamed green beans, or you could literally eat it with a spoon in a cereal bowl, like Frosted Flakes (but maybe skip the milk).

1. In a mixing bowl, whisk together the egg, 1½ tablespoons of the cornstarch, and the salt until smooth. Add the chicken and stir well to completely coat. In a separate bowl, combine the ½ cup (80g) cornstarch with the flour, then add the coated chicken and stir until the chicken is totally covered in the flour.

2. In a 2-quart (1.9L) saucepan, heat the 1½ cups vegetable oil to about 350°F (175°C). Fry the chicken in four batches, 3 to 5 minutes each, until golden brown on the outside and not at all pink on the inside. Adjust the heat as needed to maintain 350°F (175°C). Drain the chicken on a paper towel–lined plate.

3. Next, in a sauté pan large enough to comfortably hold all of the chicken you just fried, heat the remaining 2 tablespoons vegetable oil over medium-high heat until smoking. Add the garlic and cook until browned, about 5 minutes. Turn off the heat and add the scallions, grapefruit zest, grapefruit juice, maple syrup, vinegar, rosemary, peppercorns, and sesame oil, being careful of any splattering, and whisk until thoroughly mixed.

4. In a small mixing bowl, combine the stock and remaining 1 tablespoon cornstarch and whisk until the cornstarch is completely dissolved. Add the slurry to the pan, turn the heat to high, add the fried chicken pieces, and cook the chicken and sauce together, stirring occasionally, until the liquid comes to a boil, thickens, and completely glazes the chicken. Serve hot with cooked quinoa and lightly steamed green beans.

Lemony Spaghetti with Parmesan Popcorn Chicken

Serves 4

1½ cups (90g) panko bread crumbs

1½ ounces (40g) Parmesan, finely grated, plus more for serving

1 teaspoon dried oregano

½ teaspoon garlic powder

½ teaspoon ground coriander

3 teaspoons kosher salt

2 eggs

3 tablespoons cornstarch

1½ pounds (680g) boneless, skinless chicken breasts or thighs, cut into ½-inch (1.3cm) chunks

1½ cups (360ml) vegetable oil, for frying

2 tablespoons extra-virgin olive oil

8 garlic cloves, smashed

1 cup (240ml) chicken stock

1 tablespoon lemon zest, plus ¼ cup (60ml) freshly squeezed lemon juice

1 tablespoon unsalted butter

1 pound (450g) spaghetti

½ cup (10g) fresh basil leaves, torn

Red pepper flakes, for serving (optional)

I put chicken nuggets on spaghetti because, yes, I am a monster. Recently I was thinking about spaghetti pangrattato, a simple preparation that involves lemon, Parmesan, garlicky bread crumbs, and maybe a fried egg, which all send pasta over the moon. I could've just stopped there, but do you know what would really send that pasta over the moon and beyond the known universe? Using the bread crumbs, Parmesan, and garlic to form a crust around *chicken*, which we will fry and stick on top. I'm not sure what lies beyond the expanse of space, but if it isn't this nugget-topped spaghetti, then it's probably a whole lot of meaningless nothing, so I choose to believe in this spaghetti.

1. In a mixing bowl, combine the panko, 1 ounce (30g) of the Parmesan, the oregano, garlic powder, coriander, and 1 teaspoon of the salt. In a separate bowl, combine the eggs and cornstarch and whisk thoroughly. Season the chicken with 1 teaspoon of the salt, add it to the bowl with the egg mixture, and toss, coating it well. Pull out a small handful of the chicken and drain any excess dredging liquid. Toss the drained chicken in the panko mixture, breading it well. Transfer to a plate and repeat with the remainder.

2. Bring a stockpot of water to a boil over high heat to cook the pasta.

3. In a 2-quart (1.9L) saucepan, heat the vegetable oil to 350°F (175°C). Fry the chicken in four batches, for 3 to 5 minutes each, until it's not at all pink on the inside and has a golden-brown crust. Carefully remove the chicken with a slotted spoon and drain it on a paper towel–lined plate.

4. In a large sauté pan with high sides, add the olive oil and garlic and cook over medium heat until the garlic is very brown, 8 to 10 minutes. Add the stock, lemon zest, butter, and remaining 1 teaspoon salt and increase the heat to high. Bring to a boil, turn the heat to low, and simmer.

5. Cook the spaghetti in the pot of boiling water for two-thirds of the instructed time. Drain it, reserving 2 cups (480ml) of the pasta cooking liquid, and add the pasta to the sauté pan. Increase the heat to high and boil until the pasta is fully cooked. You want about 1 cup (240ml) of liquid in the pan; if you need more, add the reserved pasta water, 1 tablespoon at a time. Add the lemon juice and remaining ½ ounce (10g) Parmesan and mix well. Top each serving of spaghetti with a handful of chicken nuggets, some of the basil leaves, more Parmesan, and maybe some red pepper flakes!

Cheesy Chicken Melt with All of the Onions Relish

Makes 2 giant sandwiches, enough for 2 adults or 4 chicken-loving kids

4 teaspoons vegetable oil

2 boneless, skinless chicken breasts, about 1 pound (450g), sliced lengthwise into 4 flat ½-inch-thick (1.3cm-thick) pieces

1 teaspoon kosher salt

½ yellow onion, sliced

1 teaspoon distilled white vinegar

½ red onion, thinly sliced

½ bunch scallions, white and green parts, thinly sliced

2 tablespoons fried shallots (store-bought is totally great)

3 tablespoons salted butter

4 slices rye bread

4 slices good melting cheese, such as Colby Jack or Muenster

I have never been a huge fan of patty melts, and I accept and embrace your anger at that statement. A big hunk of meat, a bunch of melted cheese, bread, and all of that butter just doesn't sound like something I really need in my life. But switch it up with some perfectly cooked chicken and throw in a big pile of caramelized onions, and all of a sudden, I am very interested in that chicken melt sandwich. After making the components of the sandwiches and the sandwiches themselves (all told, a one-pan affair), I recommend listening to the *Radiolab* episode about colors while making a quick and easy Thousand Island dressing (mayo, ketchup, relish, maybe a little harissa!) and dipping potato chips in the sauce to test it repeatedly.

1. Heat a large sauté pan with 2 teaspoons of the vegetable oil over high heat until it is smoking. Season the chicken with ¾ teaspoon of the salt and gently place it in the pan. Cook on one side until almost cooked all the way through, about 5 minutes. Flip the chicken and cook on the other side for about 30 seconds, or until it is no longer pink. Transfer the chicken to a plate to rest.

2. Immediately add the yellow onion and the remaining 2 teaspoons vegetable oil to the pan. Stir and cook for 5 minutes, or until the onion is dark and smells amazing but is not burnt. If it's getting too dark, lower the heat. Add the vinegar, along with the liquid that has collected on the plate where the chicken is resting, and turn the heat to low. Simmer the onion for 2 to 4 minutes, or until the liquid has evaporated. Transfer the onion to a bowl, using a rubber spatula to scrape the pan out completely. When the onion has cooled down a little, about 5 minutes, add the red onion, scallions, fried shallots, and remaining ¼ teaspoon salt and stir to combine.

3. Melt 2 tablespoons of the butter in the same pan. Lay out two slices of bread on your work surface and place a slice of cheese on each. Top each piece of cheese with half of the onions, two pieces of chicken, and another slice of cheese, and cover with another slice of bread. Place the sandwiches in the pan with the melted butter. Cook over medium heat, about 3 minutes, until the cheese on the bottom slice is melted and the bread is nicely toasted. Add the remaining 1 tablespoon butter to the pan and flip the sandwiches. Cook them for another 1 to 2 minutes, until the cheese is melted and the bottom is toasty. Remove the sandwiches from the pan, cut them in half, and insert a frilly toothpick or cocktail sword near the top in each half and serve.

Tomato-Braised Chicken Thighs with Old Bay & Potatoes

Serves 1,000 children (or just 4 to 6)

1 tablespoon
vegetable oil

4 bone-in chicken thighs,
about 1½ pounds (680g),
skin removed

1½ teaspoons Old Bay
seasoning

1½ cups (360ml) water

One 14½-ounce (411g)
can crushed tomatoes

1 pound (450g)
red potatoes, cut into
1-inch (2.5cm) chunks

3 teaspoons kosher salt

2 tablespoons strained
full-fat plain yogurt

Old Bay, a seasoning from Maryland traditionally used with seafood, is actually pretty spicy! This recipe involves just a little hint of the spice blend, as well as some yogurt to further cool things down, making this a righteous pot of stew that still has a touch of kick. Don't worry—it shouldn't put any hair on your child's chest, and if it does, I'm pretty sure we sell clippers here at Food52. Old Bay's savory celery and pepper flavors are so universally good that I find myself reaching for it all of the time to give my chicken an extra dimension of spice. This dish, where chicken and creamy red potatoes are simmered in an Old Bay–spiced tomato sauce, reminds me a little of the pollo guisado from the Dominican restaurant around the corner from my apartment (which, I'm positive, does not contain Old Bay, but I suspect they are using a bunch of celery and chiles). My point is that Old Bay can go in a lot of different directions, much more easily than you'd expect of something that's immediately associated with steamed crabs. There is probably a life lesson in there, though I'm only getting paid to talk to you about chicken.

1. In a large sauté pan or Dutch oven, heat the oil over high heat. When the oil starts to smoke, add the chicken thighs and sauté until well browned, about 5 minutes per side. Add the Old Bay, letting it toast for just a minute or so in the hot chicken fat. Add the water, tomatoes, potatoes, and salt. Stir the pot and bring the liquid back up to a simmer. Lower the heat, partially cover the pot with a lid so that even if some of the potatoes aren't totally submerged in the braising liquid they'll still steam and cook (and also because I feel like that's how my mother would do it!), and simmer the stew until the chicken and potatoes are super tender, 30 to 35 minutes.

2. At this point you can serve the stew as is, with the yogurt on the side as a garnish, but what I would do is pull the thighs out of the pot, stir the yogurt into the mixture that remains, and plate the chicken thighs with a big scoop of the saucy, stewy potatoes on top.

Chicken Hash That Is Secretly Full of Vegetables

Serves 4 to 6

10 ounces (280g) russet potatoes, peeled and cut into 1-inch (2.5cm) chunks

8 ounces (225g) white sweet potato, peeled and cut into 1-inch (2.5cm) chunks

8 ounces (225g) cassava, peeled and cut into 1-inch (2.5cm) chunks

8 ounces (225g) white acorn squash, seeded, peeled, and cut into 1-inch (2.5cm) chunks

6 ounces (170g) turnip, peeled and cut into 1-inch (2.5cm) chunks

1 teaspoon kosher salt, plus 1 tablespoon

2 pounds (900g) bone-in split chicken breasts, skin removed

3 tablespoons vegetable oil

Ketchup and mayonnaise, for serving

My mom used to make me a chicken hash that consisted solely of chopped-up chicken tenderloins sautéed with leftover boiled potatoes, and it was one of my favorite breakfasts. Betty Kord, thank you for cooking so many delicious things for me when I was a child, and I'm so sorry that I always lied about doing my homework and that I became a cook instead of a lawyer and didn't buy you a house. As I was saying, I loved my mom's chicken hash, but I realize her recipe was just appeasing my pickiness and didn't have as much nutrition as my current parent-self would want in a meal. So here I've supplemented the potatoes with ingredients that resemble potatoes—white sweet potatoes, cassava (the root of the yucca plant), white acorn squash, and turnips—but you can use any starchy vegetable, like rutabaga, winter squash, or beets, especially if you're not trying to trick anyone into liking vegetables by disguising them. I think that my daughter will grow up eating this chicken hash on the weekends. I also suspect that she won't do her homework, and if she wants to become a lawyer, she will have to be one who does good things for the world, like Alexander Hamilton or Gandhi.

1. In a stockpot, combine the russet potatoes, sweet potato, cassava, squash, and turnip, just barely cover with water, and add the 1 teaspoon salt. Bring the water to a boil over high heat, turn the heat to low, and cook until the potatoes are tender (they take the longest to cook) and a paring knife goes through them easily, about 10 minutes. Drain the veggies in a colander and let them sit to dry for about 5 minutes.

2. Heat the oven to 400°F (200°C) with a sheet pan in it.

3. In a large mixing bowl, toss together the drained veggies and chicken with the oil and remaining 1 tablespoon salt. Carefully pull the hot sheet pan out of the oven and spread out the hash in a single layer, with the vegetables surrounding the chicken. Bake for 20 minutes without disturbing it, then use a thin metal spatula to turn over the chicken and vegetables. Bake for another 20 minutes, flipping any vegetables you see getting too dark, or until everything is nice and crunchy and golden, and the chicken is not at all pink in the middle (it'll be about 155°F/70°C). Carefully remove the chicken from the bone, dice it into ½-inch (1.3cm) cubes, and mix them together with the vegetables. Serve the hash with ketchup and maybe some mayo.

Chicken & Broccoli Meatball Subs with Apple Giardiniera

Makes 4 giant sandwiches

Apple Giardiniera

1 cup (240ml) each water and rice wine vinegar

1 tablespoon kosher salt

2 teaspoons maple syrup

1 whole star anise

3 bay leaves

½ bulb fennel

2 Gala or Fuji apples

1 jalapeño, stemmed

Chicken & Broccoli Meatballs

1 head broccoli

6 garlic cloves, smashed

1 tablespoon vegetable oil

1 pound (450g) ground chicken, or 1¼ pounds (570g) boneless, skinless chicken thighs, for grinding

½ cup (30g) panko bread crumbs

1 egg

1 tablespoon grated Parmesan

1 tablespoon maple syrup

1½ teaspoons kosher salt

To Assemble

Mayonnaise

4 hero rolls, split lengthwise

¼ bunch cilantro

Growing up, my mother cooked dinner for our family most nights. On the rare occasions when my parents went out, we either ate pizza or got Chinese food. Because of this, chicken and broccoli has consistently been one of the most important relationships in my life. This sandwich harnesses that magic, tops it with a spicy apple giardiniera (an Italian relish of pickled vegetables, which you can make milder by using green bell pepper instead of jalapeño), and rounds it out with mayo and cilantro. But feel free to skip the sandwich and just eat these meatballs, an amazing snack straight out of the refrigerator.

1. To make the giardiniera, combine the water, vinegar, salt, maple syrup, star anise, and bay leaves in a small saucepan and bring to a boil over high heat. Meanwhile, thinly slice the fennel, apples, and jalapeño and place into a nonreactive container. Pour the brine over the mixture and set aside to cool. Once cool, cover and refrigerate for at least 1 hour or up to 2 weeks.

2. To make the meatballs, heat the oven to 400°F (200°C). Roughly chop the broccoli. On a rimmed sheet pan, toss together the broccoli, garlic, and oil. Roast for 15 minutes, or until the broccoli is caramelized but still crunchy.

3. Meanwhile, grind the chicken if not using preground. To grind it yourself, cut the boneless thigh meat into even 1-inch (2.5cm) pieces. Working in small batches, place it in your food processor and pulse to finely chop but avoid turning it into a mousse. Transfer the chicken to a mixing bowl.

4. Once the broccoli is caramelized, transfer it to the food processor and pulse to chop. Place it in the mixing bowl with the chicken and add the panko, egg, Parmesan, maple syrup, and salt. Mix well.

5. Grease a sheet pan with vegetable oil or cooking spray. Form 12 even meatballs, approximately 1 inch (2.5cm) in size, and spread them out on the tray. Bake for 12 to 15 minutes, flipping once halfway through, or until the meatballs are cooked through, firm to the touch, and not at all pink.

6. To assemble the subs, spread mayo on both sides of the hero rolls. Halve all of the meatballs and arrange them in the rolls. Top with a little giardiniera (avoiding the bay leaves) and a lot of cilantro, stems and all!

Thank Yous

First and foremost, I would like to thank my incredible two-year-old daughter, Barbara. Her feedback was some of the most useful I received throughout the process of writing this book. It's hard to imagine a more straightforward criticism of a recipe than to see the food you've spent hours or even days perfecting spat out onto the floor. And how she howled when I was writing and not focused on her! In the end, she really, truly liked very few of the recipes that made it into this book. But she's so cute, and I want to scream at people on the street because I love her so much.

Thanks also to my wife, Katherine, who at all times had much more, and clearly more important, work to do than to worry about my silly chicken cookbook. She pulled our screaming baby off of me to allow me to get this project done, and that alone would have been enough. But she's never been that into chicken, and yet, like a chicken-eating saint, she ate nothing else for months to help me test recipes. It felt like that movie where Seth Rogen is writing a chicken cookbook and Michelle Williams has no choice but to cheat on him, but I don't think Katherine cheated on me much, if at all. Don't worry, Katherine, we can stop eating chicken now and go back to eating beans for every meal like we did before!

My agent, Jonah Straus, is who I am referring to every time I casually mention needing to "speak to my agent" or "grab a drink with my agent" when on the inside I simultaneously feel like I'm awesome and bragging like a pompous jerk. But Jonah never makes me feel like I'm bragging because he has much more successful clients than me. Still, I want to thank him heartily for always looking out for me.

Thank you so much to Ian Knauer of The Farm Cooking School for teaching me how to kill, gut, and clean chickens. It seems creepy to say that I had a really wonderful time murdering chickens with him, but I learned a lot and it made me think a ton about what it means to kill and consume animals, and it was a super-important and enriching experience.

It's funny that people think I'm a good writer, because they've never actually seen anything I've written before it was edited. Even my emails tend to be very long and rambling, so the sixty recipes in this book started out at roughly 1,500 words each. Brinda Ayer was the editor who managed to turn it all into a coherent book. For months we had a weekly call on Tuesdays at 11 a.m., during which I would rant and rave—sometimes about chicken but more often than not about cultural appropriation, authenticity, or my own insecurities as a white man (and also as a person)—and she helped me sort through it all. Thank you so much, Brinda, these exclamation points are for you!!!!!!!!!!!!!!!!

I would also like to thank Amanda Hesser and Merrill Stubbs for seeing something in me that shouted "Chicken!" and giving me the opportunity to write this book. And Suzanne D'Amato and Kristen Miglore, thank you for not talking Amanda and Merrill out of it.

I appreciate the whole creative team at Food52, but I especially want to thank Alexis Anthony, James Ransom, Sarah Wight, Anna Billingskog, Yossy Arefi, and Josh Cohen, who were so sweet and wonderful and helpful.

And this book wouldn't exist without Julie Bennett, Emma Rudolph, Emma Campion, Lisa Bieser, Mari Gill, Serena Sigona, David Hawk, Allison Renzulli, and the rest of the team at Ten Speed Press—thank you!

Last, I would like to thank my baby, Barbara, again, because she is seriously so cute and looks enough like a chicken that we should have slipped a photo of her into the book. Next time.

Index

Published in the United States by Ten Speed Press,
an imprint of Random House, a division of
Penguin Random House LLC, New York.
www.tenspeed.com

Ten Speed Press and the Ten Speed Press colophon are
registered trademarks of Penguin Random House LLC.

Some of the materials in this work first appeared on the Food52 website.

Library of Congress Cataloging-in-Publication Data
Names: Kord, Tyler, author. | Ransom, James (Photographer), photographer.
Title: Food52 dynamite chicken : 60 never-boring recipes for your favorite
    bird / Tyler Kord ; photography by James Ransom. Other titles: Food52.
Description: California : Ten Speed, [2019] | Includes index.
Identifiers: LCCN 2019008583 | ISBN 9781524759001 (hardcover)
Subjects: LCSH: Cooking (Chicken) | LCGFT: Cookbooks.
Classification: LCC TX750.5.C45 K67 2019 | DDC 641.6/65—dc23
    LC record available at https://lccn.loc.gov/2019008583

Hardcover ISBN: 978-1-5247-5900-1
eBook ISBN: 978-1-5247-5901-8

Printed in China

Design by Lisa Bieser
Food styling by Anna Billingskog
Art direction and prop styling by Alexis Anthony

10 9 8 7 6 5 4 3 2 1

First Edition